A
SHORT INTRODUCTION
TO THE
CATHOLIC CHURCH

Severino Dianich

A Short
Introduction
to the
Catholic Church

ST PAULS

Original title: *Una Chiesa per vivere*
© Edizioni San Paolo srl, Cinisello Balsamo (Milano), Italy

Translated by Sr Frances Teresa osc

The Scripture quotations in this publication are from the Revised
Standard Version of the Bible, and are used by permission.

Cover: Giovanni B. della Porta, *Christ gives the keys to Peter*.
Church of Santa Pudenziana, Rome. Photo: Epipress – Baraontini.
By kind permission of Edizioni San Paolo srl.

ST PAULS
Middlegreen, Slough SL3 6BT, United Kingdom
Moyglare Road, Maynooth, Co. Kildare, Ireland

© ST PAULS (UK) 1994

ISBN 085439 490 7

Set by TuKan, High Wycombe

Printed by The Guernsey Press Co., Guernsey, C.I.

ST PAULS is an activity of the priests and brothers of the
Society of St Paul who proclaim the Gospel through the media
of social communication

Contents

Foreword

This little book on the Catholic Church is designed to be read by all kinds of people, but primarily by those who do not see themselves as theologians.

Theology is a true study in its own right. It is an almost scientific discipline, like history, philosophy, literary criticism and the other subjects which are taught and studied at university. A student of theology is concerned with religious phenomena which are as historical as those studied in other disciplines, but he or she does not approach this subject from outside, as a student of social phenomena would, to whom faith is of no personal interest. The theologian studies religious phenomena from within, following the logic of a believer, not of one who has no faith. For this reason, theology is a unique kind of science, but it is a science for all that. It considers, and also stimulates, every possible question that can be put to faith by human intelligence. It therefore speaks the language of its time and culture. It has an elaborate terminology, it uses methods of rational argument, logical, unemotional and unbiased, and in general, it is difficult for those who are not trained in it.

However, what the reader will find in these pages is

not the fruit of research carried out in the shadow of a library or a theological faculty. The reader will find the fruit of an experience of the Church gained through teaching children their catechism, at the bedside of the dying, standing alongside a mother whose 20 year-old son has died. It has been forged in the hard work of many decisions made with the pastoral council, of writing sermons and preparing liturgies. In a word, it emerges from the experience of a parish priest.

Because I was, for many years, tied to teaching and study, I have often published books and articles of a specialist nature, but I have always been fired by the idea of writing something which was not just for intellectuals, theologians and university students but for the civil servant or the postal worker. Theological research should never be allowed to pile up in libraries, but should be put at the service of the Church. There it can give life to the thinking of the faithful and enter into dialogue with all those who are asking questions about the meaning of faith.

To write theology in a way that everyone can understand is no easy task. Every mechanic knows that it is far easier to explain a mechanical breakdown to one who already knows about engines than to one who has never set foot in a workshop. It is true, though, that the majority of readers of this book will be those who do set foot in Church and – at least occasionally – go to Mass. However, it is possible to be a very committed Christian and yet to be starved, theologically speaking, especially if we are not in the habit of asking ourselves questions or have never made any effort to find answers to the questions our intelligence puts to our faith.

The faithful often suspect a theologian of being someone with a critical turn of mind who loves to churn up the calm waters of faith. He or she is some-one to whom all sorts of queries are put or occur, which (in his or her mind at least) merit serious study. From such studies come a continuous flow of paper about what the Church is to believe and do. Such is the popular view of theologians. Would it not be better for us, people say, to ignore the doubts and questions and carry on as we always have done? But a theologian seeks to understand and, above all, to bring the intelligence of today's men and women to bear on matters of faith. So for this reason, a theologian always hopes to contribute to that constant evolution of the Church which is essential (*pace* those who want nothing changed) if we are to keep seeking how to be ever more faithful to Jesus Christ.

Chapter one

What people say

Let us begin by summarising the most obvious difficulties and problems. What do people think about the Church? The press and so-called lay opinion, who consider themselves outside the Church (and therefore, who judge the Church from outside) often have very decided ideas about it. The faithful are usually less decided because their experience of the Church is more varied and more vital. The others, though, are like people living in a very small house into which every expression of the wider Church has to fit. If you say or do anything which does not find a place in their scheme of things you will soon find yourself told that you are no longer a true Catholic. Naturally, when this happens, it does not mean that the journalists are bad or ignorant people but only that, in order to understand the Church properly, one must be inside it.

Also, of course, the Church too sometimes makes mistakes about the way it presents itself to the world, and once a deformed picture has been transmitted, it is very difficult to remove it from circulation again.

We have only to turn on the television to see the figure of the Pope, often side by side with the faces of those who wield power over people. It is not uncommon to see him at some airport, welcomed like a Head of State with fanfares and the playing of bands, with the military passing in review before him. This is why the Church looks to many people just like another State, and of course, there is still the Vatican City State with its own band and its own car registration, SCV: Stato della Città del Vaticano.

The Pope, indeed, is more or less like a king or a head of government. The Church has its politics and must be judged by them. It is not for nothing that the Church has ambassadors to various governments, and representatives at international organisations, and a certain bargaining power on the world stage. For many, this image of the Church overshadows its actual credibility. Politics, as we say, is a dirty game. Yet, over and above this prejudice, which is deeply rooted and widespread, there is also a genuine need to make a true and accurate assessment of the political policies of the Church. The problem is whether or not these serve the cause of peace, whether or not they strengthen humanity's aspirations towards justice and freedom.

Until a few years ago, the general opinion was that Vatican policies had a 'conservative' orientation. 'The Church is right-wing.' For reasons to do with history and tradition, the Church was seen as the enemy of, in opposition to, all that was new, whether the new was the French Revolution at the end of the eighteenth century or the socialist revolution in Russia at the beginning of this century, a revolution which gave birth to the communist regimes of the east.

This constant struggle against communism and the very bitter and cruel persecution which the Church experienced in return, left it closed to any manifestations of the political left. As a result, the workers of the world suffered a widespread and deep loss of confidence in the Church. Today in this area, many things are changing. The great communist dream of social regeneration is breaking up. The policies of the Pope and the Vatican with regard to the great themes of war and peace, their support for Third World countries, their promotion of human rights and their defence of the oppressed are so marked as to be recognised by everyone.

However, notwithstanding all this, the riches of the Vatican and the splendour of its works of art, the consideration the powerful show towards the dignitaries of the Church, the Pope's frequent public appearances with Heads of State and governments, all these things help to nourish an attitude of caution or suspicion towards the Church. It seems hard to discern in all these things, a continuation of the work of Jesus, who lived humbly and vulnerably, always surrounded by poor people. If we add to all this certain financial adventures in which, guilty or otherwise, the Vatican has become implicated, we complete the picture of a Church which is not much loved by large sectors of our society.

On the other hand, of course, there are plenty of people who do greatly admire the Church, and these include both believers and non-believers. They have confidence in the role which the Church's current policies give her on the world scene. They are not amazed when they see the Pope, cardinals or bishops accompanied by the powerful of the earth. In fact, they consider that in this way, and only in this way, can the

Church pursue her mission for the good of everyone.

All the same, it is not our intention to pass judgement on this showy aspect of the Church. What is important is to ask whether this is the truest and deepest meaning of the word Church – and the answer to that is clear. This is not the whole Church nor is the Church principally this. The Church is not simply the Vatican, nor is the Pope the only one responsible for the Church's political line. Any well-informed Catholic knows well that the Vatican, its ambassadors and its political alliances with governments could very well be changed without the Church thereby being diminished or the Pope becoming any less important.

It is understandable that in so complex a reality there should be superficial and ostentatious aspects which offend the sensibilities of those who observe the Church from outside. Such people should take into account that the great relevance of the Church on the world stage does not come from the existence of the Vatican State. If the value of the Church resided in its territory, armed forces or finance, then the Vatican State would be of very little interest to anyone, for the same reason that the daily papers do not say much about, say, Andorra or San Marino. It is obvious that within the Vatican and its politics there is a far greater reality at work, and this is the Church in the fullest meaning of the word. That reality is an immense gathering of believers who are recognised by their shared faith and who are to be found in innumerable communities scattered all around the world.

Again, the 900 million Christians who say that they belong to the Roman Catholic Church are not citizens of the Vatican State. They pay no taxes, they are obliged to no military service in defence of Vatican boundaries. They belong to the Church from choice and are as involved as they choose to be. The Vatican is no White House, no Number 10 Downing Street. The Church does not govern people and nations by means of imposed laws, nor has it the power to enforce the observance of such laws.

The truth is that those who live as members of the Church know only too well that they are not subjects of the Vatican. It is only from outside the Church that anyone thinks of it as a kind of highly disciplined structure in which the Pope and Vatican organisations send out commands that are instantly carried out all over the world. In reality, believers may or may not approve of the Vatican; they can and should debate the Vatican's political line. It is for historical reasons that the Vatican is a State and the Holy See enjoy good international standing in law; and this is a fact which could develop in the future or indeed be completely changed. There is no doubt about it: in order to understand the Church, one should not start with the Vatican. The Church is a gathering of people, experiences, traditions and institutions. The Vatican is among these, but only as one among thousands of other aspects, none of which have anything to do with the nature or politics of the Vatican.

Priests and bishops

There are very many people who pay little attention to the political aspect, people to whom the Church is simply an affair of priests and bishops, mitres and tonsures, sacristies and convents, far more than simply the Vatican. Within this varied complex of people and institutions there is no lack of personalities and initiatives which are greatly respected and trusted. All this happens in spite of the sort of clerical cast system with which the Church is often identified and as a result of which the Church has often been surrounded with a certain vague suspicion. The reality is that those who look at this from outside should not expend their energy on an apparatus which is, of its nature, only concerned with the internal life of the Church and which only affects those who want to be part of the Catholic community.

Although the thing looks so simple, the reality is rather more complex than it appears. To take Italy as an example, notwithstanding the fact that only about 25 per cent of the population go to Mass on Sundays, there are many more who consider themselves bound in one way or another to the Church. It is doubtful whether they would profess a devoted obedience to the bishops, but they do create an impression that Italy is a Catholic country. This gives rise to the idea that every citizen must inevitably have some dealings with the Church, as if it were a structural component of civil society. For many, even among non-believers, the priests and bishops are seen as one of the many State organisations, like the judiciary, the police and the teachers. In fact, rather like the judiciary, priests have to be above party politics. 'The Church has no political party' is a kind of undisputed dogma. So it only needs a bishop to utter one word on some problem outside the strictly religious field for there to be a violent reaction. The Church is seen as a hidden force which, under the cloak of religion, shifts the balance in favour or this or that but never, so it is said, in favour of democracy or freedom.

It is very easy to read all this in terms of power politics and many, confronted with the Church, instinctively adopt a defensive attitude which certainly does nothing for calm debate and openness between those engaged in confrontation. Given this situation, Christ is sometimes hardly seen over the horizon of the Church.

Those who go to church

Sometimes, though maybe not often, when we speak of the Church we mean, not the Pope, the Vatican, the priests and bishops, but the ordinary people who believe in the Church, who love it and live by it. We see, and make judgements about, those who go to Mass each Sunday, who co-operate with the parish priest and join associations and movements with a Catholic ethic.

Some may have met Catholics dedicated to prayer, who go on spiritual retreats, who spend hours and hours in meditation on Holy Scripture and in discussions of a spiritual nature. It is not easy to enter into their search, or even simply to understand what they are about. They speak a language all their own, full of Biblical terminology. Their lives are governed by the rules of their group which make it difficult when they come to communicate with other Catholics or their friends. Their experience seems to alienate them from this concrete world in which ordinary, everyday life is lived. If this is the Church, people say, then it is out of this world.

Others contrariwise, may have encountered of much more combative Catholics who concern themselves about specific problems of a public nature. These people are not content just with prayer and spiritual withdrawal. They want to intervene in things with all their energy and to attain their goals by whatever means will be most successful. This kind of Catholic re-awakens the spectre of the clerical Church with little respect for civil society or the lay nature of the State. From this perspective, many see the Church as a dangerous rival which must be combated in order to save true democracy and rescue the free and up-to-date character of our society.

Finally, the popular and most accessible view of the Church is that of the normal parish in the city or out in the country, where people work together with the parish priest and attendance at religious functions is normal. Often those who stand outside parish life are very severe judges of the practising Catholic. There is a sentence often heard on their lips: 'I am more Christian than those who go to Church.' When we consider the witness to the world of practising Christians, then the gaps and contradictions are obvious to all. Christianity can seem nothing more than a tired religious tradition, often mixed up with superstition, supported by ignorance, holding together these groups of Catholics who think they have done all when they have said the rosary and muttered a few more prayers. It is even worse when they happen to meet that particular kind of Catholic who, in the witty expression of one writer: 'in a procession, hold up their head as if it were the Blessed Sacrament itself'. Such people show their belonging to the Church in such a way as to make it a springboard for any fragment of glory or chance of publicity that might be going.

The result of such comments and judgements is that many refuse, even though they seriously cherish religious aspirations, to take any real part in the life of the community. They are happy just to skim along with a desultory presence at religious festivals, and so they never have any adequate experience of what the Church really is, either in her defects or in the deeper dimensions of her life.

Good and bad reasons

Those who live as members of the Church with sincere faith know only too well that criticism and suspicions are often founded on hard fact. The Pope knows the burden of the Vatican better than anyone, nor are the bishops unaware of that some of them have taken up an ambiguous position in civil life. People in the Church know what they call their 'sins' even better than those outside do, and every Christian community is conscious of the weight of its own inconsistencies. At every Mass, the Church begins by beating its breast and asking God and humanity for forgiveness for all those thoughts, words, deeds and omissions.

The problem, however, is bigger than that. Even if the Church were sinless and wholly unambiguous, it would still find itself judged and condemned by the world. We have only to recall the fact that many people think it is absurd to believe in God and quite irrational to put our trust in Christ. They consider it an illusion, a flight from the real problems of life. Or, according to some, the phenomenon of religion is there to lay a respectable mantle over hidden interests which really have nothing to do with God and Christ and which must therefore be unmasked. When this turns out not to be so, then they decide that it must be the fruit of a certain psychological immaturity.

Marxism was atheist in ideology, but today's dominant middle class mentality is atheist in practice. There is a whole attitude to life in which up faith is in money, with a sacred respect for the laws of economy and a

19

fatalism that simply accepts exploitation and wars. It includes an individualistic concept of freedom, the loss of vision and hope on the part of many, along with many other attitudes of mind which are decidedly contrary to that of the Gospel. For this middle class mentality, the world, society and history have nothing to learn from anyone's religious convictions, nor do they welcome anything which leads them from their chosen path. Believers may think as they choose in private life, but as citizens, politicians, civil servants, economists, scholars, health workers and so on, they must act as if they had no faith. They dare not speak of God in public, nor try to apply the criteria of the Gospel to secular society.

The marginalisation of faith in our society has, without doubt, a certain historical justification in the memory of the religious intolerance practised by the Church in the past. From one point of view, the Church itself has sometimes favoured the idea that faith is a private problem. In fact, it has seemed to some that the Christian message calls us exclusively to save our own soul for eternal life. The good Christian has no concern with the good of society. Everything happens within the Church and the home, it is quite enough if such a person conducts himself or herself with honesty, if he or she prays, obeys the authorities, frequents the sacraments and thus gains sufficient merit to go to Paradise.

Marxism, which has conducted a long and bitter struggle against religion in general and the Church in particular, seems, for the moment, to have lost its vigour. Our inheritance from Marxism has been that we have acquired a mind-set in which all human reality is ultimately explained by the economy. The conflict of interests determines life's development; then, if we are to understand the reality of whatever happens, we must first ask questions about its economic structure. Even the facts of religion do not escape this law; if there are people who believe in God, if the Church exists, then we must look behind appearances and beyond the most sincere convictions of believers. This attitude of looking beyond does, in fact, make people much more able to endure the sufferings of life and therefore it renders a great service to all exploiters because it gives the exploited the hope of eternal life and thus extinguishes any desire they might have for rebellion.

On the other hand, it is also true that a Church which is only concerned with calling people to prayer and good works, soon finds, for the same reason, that the more vulnerable members of society have been left in the hands of the dominant power. It buys the favours from the regime in this way, as well as being conceded certain privileges and legislation in line with Catholic moral teaching, particularly in matters of sexuality. However, it insults the intelligence if every twig is made into a stick with which to beat the Church, especially in a history as long and complex as this one. Nor can we forget that it was Christianity which first introduced a liberation movement into the resigned climate of pagan fatalism. Admittedly, there have been long periods in the history of Christianity marked by popes and bishops who were preoccupied with power and money rather than the Gospel. In more recent times, it has also been the case that the personal holiness and good faith of many ecclesiastics has not been adequate to the task of understanding the new times and the genuine values of those times.

As you see, the reasons why the Church is attacked by the world of today are many and weighty. We always need to know how to discern when, on the one hand, authentic Christian values are concerned and are being sought within the Church, and when, on the other hand, the Church is being called – at whatever cost – to stand against the world and confront it with the new power of the Gospel.

Chapter two

How it looks from the inside

Let us go round the streets and bars and listen to those outside the Church, let us hear what they are saying about it. Then we shall go inside and see what those think about it who, in a manner of speaking, consider it theirs and regard it as home.

That was my Grandad

In general, young people long for novelty while old folk like tradition. However, there are situations in life where the search for novelty is onerous and tiring. Also, even young people follow the route which seems the easier, the one others have taken and which they are used to. Many young people when they come to the age when they have to choose which party to vote for, end up by voting the same way as their parents. Similarly, when they come to marriage, quite a few of them choose a religious wedding. This is not because they really believe but because it is still the normal way of getting married, the way which causes the least speculation and the least reaction from their relatives and home background.

This drifting way of behaving is determined by a certain inner laziness, but also, whether we like it or not, there does exist a kind of spiritual inheritance of ideas and values from which we draw certain things to which we remain attached all our lives. This does not indicate any profound conviction, only a strong attachment. Imagine a chap, long estranged from the Church, who takes out of his bag an ancient crucifix, greasy and filthy, that his mother had given him when he joined up, and declares that he would never get rid of it for anything in the world. The Church is like this for many. It is the traditional religion received from their parents and to be passed on to their children. They come seeking baptism for their children and say 'My grandparents and my parents were Christians, my child must be too.' Motivation like this does not do much for a punctilious fulfilment of religious commitment. These people are married in church, have their grandparents buried there, seek baptism for their children, bring them up for their first Communion and Confirmation, ask for their houses to be blessed. A furtive sign of the cross, rather like the sign to avert the evil eye; certain specific occasions like Christmas and Easter Mass, all heard from a place as near the door as possible, these are the only remaining indications of belonging to a Church which they have no intention of completely renouncing. This way of being a Christian is, for many people, almost part of good manners, necessary if the family is to retain its good name. Anything more would be called bigotry, anything less would be to live like an animal.

The phenomenon which we are describing is consistent though diffuse, and in recent years appears to be in decline. For a Church which wants to survive, the immediate temptation must surely be to give a decisive shake-up to this kind of religious world, setting it free with powerful gestures. The temptation is to deny the sacraments to those who fail to show serious belief and who are reluctant to shoulder the burdens of Christian community life. At first glance such a clean sweep would rejuvenate the Church. It would find itself much reduced in numbers but with a completely new face and an ability to attract which would be infinitely more effective than at present.

It would be advantageous. But would it be honest? Perhaps not. So far the Church has preserved its position as the legitimate expression of the religious feeling and integrity of the people. Even today many Catholics are not at all disposed to offer respect and a welcoming friendship to those who have broken off contact with the Church. Yet it is unjust to claim that we adhere to a faith that is free, convinced and committed while, at the same time, we do not guarantee respect and consideration for those who make different choices in the matter of public morals. We will not be able to resolve the problems of conventional religion until the whole Church – bishops, priests and faithful – is unwilling to accept, maybe with legitimate sorrow but without being scandalised, those who profess atheism or seek an altogether different faith. Only a spirit of toleration without reproach, only the creation of a new mind-set in which the greatest good is the freedom of every conscience – only those will grant the Church the right to free itself from the dead weight of a tradition which denies the free choice of faith. Instead, tradition tends to substitute chains stained with blood and the inertia of social custom. Besides, we would be in danger of throwing out the baby with the bath water. Nobody knows how the Spirit is moving people's hearts, even under the most superficial appearances, behind the roughest expression of Christian commitment.

Christian nomads

One of the more serious signs of belonging to the Church is the habitual attendance at Sunday Mass. There are Christians who make very small demands on the Church, who seem able to find all they need for the honesty and faith of their own consciences. At the same time, they realise that there is something which only the Church can give: the sacraments. Jesus himself willed that faith should be accompanied by baptism, the Christian life by Mass and Holy Communion, penitence by confession of sins and so on. The sacraments are a gift from above, mysterious and indispensable. Christ, who willed this, has created the priesthood of the Church as the means by which the sacraments can be administered. The Church is indispensable for this, yet at the same time, the Church is not very important. It is indispensable because only in the Church do we find the mystery of the sacraments; it is not very important because the mystery is far greater than the instrument, the Church.

For many, however, it does not matter who the priest is that says Mass, nor the community who stand before the altar. Mass is intrinsically valuable, simply because of the mystery of Christ's presence. So they choose the church where the time of Mass is more convenient, wandering here and there, Sunday after Sunday. Sometimes they go where there is a good programme of organ music or, quite simply, where the

Mass is quicker. On the whole, this kind of Christian likes a basic liturgy, where no demand is made for a participation which might be personal or instructive, where everyone says his or her own prayers and receives the sacrament in private, and ignores all those who are standing nearby. Naturally they are greatly scandalised if the priest in his sermon dares to touch on any debate which might concern them, or demand that they make some concrete change in their lives. They prefer him to make a few observations of a general nature, which satisfy their critical sense without disturbing their genuine interest in no-one but themselves.

Faith in the sacraments touches on the most valuable things in the Church. The truth is that what has supported the Church through the darkest moments of loss has only been that gift which, in spite of all else, rests in its hands; the gift of bread which is the Body of Christ. Yet paradoxically, it is exactly this which many cannot accept. They say: 'Why should I impose a religious institution and a prescribed cult between me and God?' If we reply that Christ wanted it this way, they may agree but may also add that that is not an explanation. Then they might press the matter further: 'And why should Christ, who so stressed the interiority of the conscience, have linked salvation to the celebration of a ritual?' We reply that Jesus wanted there to be the sacraments and this is why he established the Church. But the opposite could also be true, that he wanted there to be the Church and that is why he made the sacraments. In order to understand the sacraments, we need to discover a sense of the Church, rather than vice versa.

No man is an island. We live with others in order to work together. We make friends in order to have fun together. We seek good companions to study with us. We fall in love and commit ourselves to a life together. So, for those who believe in God, we also live together as part of our faith experience. With this perspective, there is no great questioning of the existence of the Church, because the Church is more like the air we breathe. If things do not go well, then we suffer terribly and this is always a sign that we are dealing with something integral to our lives, something about which we feel deeply.

It all begins when we seriously want to believe in Jesus, to know him and to some extent to find him. Jesus is not an embalmed mummy, he is not like a photograph in a history book depicting some bust of Julius Caesar. To meet Jesus is to live in a new atmosphere, which is him, himself, alive. This is hard to explain to anyone who has not experienced it, but a meeting with Jesus is a whole way of life. Then even the Gospel which you read and the Communion you receive are not enough, they are only isolated moments which of themselves have nothing to say to you. This is how you realise that what you have with other believers is not just a shared religion or some rituals or a profession of faith. It is a shared life. My life in Christ permeates yours, yours is mingled with mine. Together we have this adventure of discovering Jesus. From the threads of the Gospel we weave the fabric of our friendship. The personality of the Christian develops through these intertwining relationships.

However, there is a danger in this view of Christ, which is that of making him into a sort of warm refuge where we can hide ourselves from the hardness of life and the conflicts which divide society. There are in fact Christians who live out their lives exactly as if they were lost in some strange land and they only feel themselves at home with the Christian community. Now, the Church is indeed a place in which to live but only within the wider context of the life of the world. The Church is like a house which has neither doors nor windows. In the Christian experience as it is lived within a community, we concentrate the best of what we are and the best of our belief. But this is like the rhythm of the heart or of any other organism: there is contraction and expansion, tension and relaxation. An ancient and famous saying defines the Church as the soul of the world – fine, but the soul permeates the body.

Not without difficulty

The truth is that we cannot invite anyone into the Church without showing them the contradictions they will have to encounter. This is not simply a matter of the hard work involved in being consistent, a matter which is always the price of following any chosen ideal. There are also some problems inherent in the nature of the Church which are felt today with particular keenness and which sometimes make it seem impossible to come up with a satisfactory solution.

The Church, in fact, is born from faith, and faith is an interior act, entirely free and personal, flowing from spontaneous inspiration and from the unique quality of each person's conscience. This kind of thing also happens to those who fall in love and wish to marry. Love is the ultimate form of freedom, spontaneity, self-generating enthusiasm; love is new every day, and unpredictable. To marry is to commit oneself to life with another, to assume the future responsibilities of children, to bind oneself to a stable and constant pattern of life. And will that not be the end of all spontaneity in love? So faith is an entering into God, moving in infinite space. Nothing gives such a sensation of freedom or passion for liberty as faith in Jesus. But someone will say: "Why must I hide in a Church? It seems like hiding in some convent, making myself the slave of a new social system. I will have to deal with the clergy, with presumptuous and authoritarian bishops, go to Mass on Sundays, go to confession, subject myself to a stale and narrow-minded morality, lose my freedom of opinion." Will it prove true that marriage is the tomb of love and the Church the tomb of God?

There is another problem. In the eyes of faith, God is the most important reality of life. So true is this that there are those who enclose themselves in monasteries in order to dedicate themselves wholly to God and are convinced that this is not a waste of their lives. On the other hand, the Christian faith is also a message of salvation to be taken out to the whole world. How can we reconcile these two extremes? Liturgy and contemplation, singing and prayer, incense smoke, lace and flowers, trappings and bowings, the whole atmosphere of the Church, all carry us out of this world. They create another world for us as if we already lived in God. On the other hand, if someone wants to live by the Gospel and serve others through work, trade unions and politics, then they must ask how all these things can help their faith. An effective economic and political programme which, in a concretely realisable manner, looks towards a future of good living on a basis of justice, freedom and progress, is surely enough in itself. To offer a valid salvation to the world, must one make the sign of the cross and whisper prayers?

There is a third problem. The Gospel is very demanding, it is impossible to live up to its ideals perfectly. To some extent, every Christian is bound to be counterfeit. Better, surely, to be honest enough not to undertake so elevated a way of life rather than adopt a flag and dishonour it? The Gospel is like the constitution of the Church. The Church preaches the Gospel and says: You must act justly, bring about peace, throw your arms away, help the developing nations. You must do this and this and this...! But is this what the Church actually does? The sincere Christian experiences these questions as a personal problem. They cannot offload them onto the Pope or the Vatican or the structures; they must carry them around and be constantly tormented by them. It seems to many people that it would be better to have more modest ideals with less ambition to change the world, and to have a theory and practice which were more consistent with each other. Better to keep away from these chosen people and make the best one can of oneself, having one's own standards and living up to them.

Finally, there is the knotty problem of politics. Many ethical questions, such as those surrounding abortion or euthanasia, have political implications. Faced with such questions, no thinking Christian would dare to say that their faith has nothing to do with how they exercise their political responsibility. Indeed, the Christian conscience is very involved in many questions to which the believing citizen has to respond with some definite choice, and in the end, that choice is made concrete at the polling station.

Given the enormous diversification of ethical and political problems, together with the difficulty of putting forward political projects which are global as well as realisable, it is very difficult for any one political party to guarantee respect for the catholic conscience, certainly not to such an extent that the faithful can put their whole trust in the party's decisions. It would seem necessary therefore for Catholics to be militants within their chosen political party, to keep alive an awareness of faith and moral conscience, and in this way to exercise a serious and unremittingly critical role. Following the Gospel must flow even into the political choices we make, but no political choice can do more than constantly submit itself to the judgement of the Gospel.

So we can conclude that the Church is not an oasis of peace! The Church is an adventure, a splendid adventure, an adventure for the whole of life. Only the stupid know no difficulties and only the foolish have no doubts. The Church lives with one certitude: Jesus is risen. The greater this certainty becomes, the more we can allow ourselves to live in uncertainty, to travel gropingly, to feel our way forward by finding the footprints of God in the world.

Chapter three

A fact: the birth of the Church

The Church is old; everyone knows that – almost 2,000 years old. It seems impossible that the Church should not be there. This would be like thinking of the horizon with no mountains on it, or of the sky with no puff of cloud. Even the great political leaders have usually preferred to tie the Church to their service rather than attempt to destroy it.

Threads of freedom

Still, the existence of the Church, if we think about it, hangs on a thread. In this respect, the Church can be contrasted with the secular state. Any kind of society without the State would, in fact, be unthinkable. We may destroy one form of the State, but it is only in order to give shape and substance to another form. So, of its nature, the institution of a State has a stability far greater than that of the Church, whose life hangs on the thread of a believer's act of faith. Drag our toes as we will, emigrate and promote revolution as we may, we cannot, by a simple act of will, destroy our belonging to the State. Yet this can happen with the Church at any moment. The Church exists only in so far as, and only when, there are people who belong to it, and who are part of it by their free adherence in faith. Let us suppose that at a given moment, all the faithful freely ceased to believe: at that moment the Church would automatically cease to exist. So for this reason, we can never say that the Church exists, Amen: this is quite different from saying that there is a pine tree in front of my house and mountains behind it. No, the Church is always something which happens, while remaining something which could cease to happen.

How a Church is born

I have never watched a Church develop from nothing and I think there are very few Christians who have. Even the missions in Africa and Asia consist often, it seems, of existing communities in which the children are baptised as Christians and educated in Catholic schools. The arrival of new believers is often more like an organic growth than a new creature in any way.

Let us have a flight of fancy here. What would it be like if there were no Christianity? Let us think for a moment of a world without Christians, without priests, without cathedrals, without the Gospel. Then imagine that, at a particular moment, someone comes along who does believe in Jesus. He sets himself to tell us about his own experience in faith. He tells us who Jesus is, what it means to believe in him and what changed in his own life when he began to believe. It could then happen that someone else begins to show a deeper interest in what he or she hears, and finally

34

decide that he or she, too, want to share this faith experience. At that point, the Church is born. In other words, you have people of the same faith experience following the call of the Gospel together. This would be a beginning, like the germination of a seed. It still needs consolidation, it still needs to be articulated throughout all its structures. This is the first germinating of the plant, but branches and leaves have yet to come. Yet within the seed, all is present. Such a moment would be an authentic birth of the Church.

We need to imagine that kind of beginning because the experience usually comes to us within a Church that has already been well and truly planted, back in the past. On the other hand, if we think about it, such a scenario happens among us all the time because, although we may baptise our children, they are not Christians by baptism but by faith. And faith is never a matter simply of putting a gift down on the table and that is enough. Faith is a free choice. In the same way, the act of faith never sprouts in the human spirit on its own but always arises out of a meeting with others who believe.

To sum up, nobody believes by nature. Nobody becomes a believer all alone. The Church is a free union of people who, by communicating their faith to others, find themselves sharing an experience of Christ. This union is as profound as the faith they bring to it. It is then no longer enough to call it 'union'; we must in fact call it 'communion'.

It all began with that piece of news

For the Church to be born, the one thing necessary is the word. Everything begins when one person com-

35

municates to another the news of Jesus, and we know that 'Gospel' in Greek means 'Good news'. So we can understand why it is that, on the political level, the Church is most alarming to those authoritarian regimes who take away freedom of speech.

It is not easy to find people who have never heard anything about Jesus. They have heard, at least, that he was born in poverty at Bethlehem, they have heard of his preaching about love, of his death by crucifixion. Most of these things are widely known. Some people with good memories can even recall a mass of information from the catechism, ranging from the account of creation to the doctrine of the Trinity, from the ten commandments to the virginity of Mary, from the indissolubility of marriage to stories about David. We old-style Christians have the disadvantage that we have experienced a faith communication which had, perhaps, the defect of too much information – and this makes it difficult for us to adopt the true heart of the Good News as our own.

We must call on our imagination for help. If we were at rock bottom and someone came to speak to us about Christ, what is the first thing he or she would tell us? Surely, the first thing is that Christ was killed because of what he preached and, absolutely uniquely and miraculously, rose again. This is the crux of our faith and all the rest depends on it. If Christ is risen, then I can take him as my Saviour. He is the hope of all the world because he is the only one who has risen from the dead. So I can also adore him as my God, indeed as a God of love who will give my life a future. In order to express the absolute sense in which he is the first, the number one of life, the early Christians used to cry out: "Jesus is Lord!" This is the first creed of the Church.

Everyone wants to know how to live his or her life, how to expend his or her energy. Jesus spent his for the good of others. He had a precise and concrete agenda, but although he gave without recompense, he did not give without hope. Christ on the cross is a clamorous sign of failure: 'You see what happens if you go round doing good to others.' If Jesus is risen then by being condemned to the cross he became for the world the most powerful burden of love ever to disturb the course of history.

For those inside: a mystery of God

Without doubt, anyone who tells the news about Jesus today and fills another with enthusiasm, who creates between them the bond of this exceptional and overwhelming hope, such a person has certainly done a great work. This is not only so for those who look in from the outside of the Church, but also for those who live on the inside, who hold fast to the Christian way of life. Indeed, it is only from within the immense wonder of the Church that one can measure the absolutely unique quality of that which happened. St Paul wrote to the Christians at Corinth: 'in Christ Jesus... in every way you were enriched in him' (1 Cor 1:4-5). And then, in his second letter: 'if any one is in Christ, he is a new creation: the old has passed away, behold, the new has come' (2 Cor 5:17). The great new thing is that Christ has risen from the dead. This is not something which only concerns him, it is a quantum leap for the life of us all and for the course of history.

Those who believe know only too well that this new experience which they live is due to no merit of theirs. The incredible news, and the vigour of soul needed to

37

accept it, both come from God who moves us from within in the direction of faith. St Paul states this quite clearly: 'No one can say: "Jesus is Lord!" except the Holy Spirit' (1 Cor 12:3). Viewed from within, this event is experienced as a mysterious presence of God, it is the Holy Spirit bringing the Church into being by moving the hearts of believers from within and drawing them together.

The union between the Church and its founder Jesus is also unique. To give an example, many streets, buildings and institutions are named after figures from our history. The intention is, perhaps, to inspire us to remember and follow their example. The Church, however, does not call on characters out of history, no matter how much they have determined our present, because the fact is that they belong to the past. In the Church, we call ourselves Christians and gather round Jesus Christ, not just in the strength of his memory but because we are convinced that he is a living person, present among us. One of Christ's sayings most dear to the Church is given in chapter 18 of St Matthew's Gospel: "where two or three are gathered in my name, there am I in the midst of them" (Mt 18:20).

In the risen Jesus, who is alive in those who believe, the Church becomes – as every Christian knows – something far greater than just a historical foundation begun by someone in the remote past. God is found. So our understanding grows and is enriched. Jesus, in fact, is not simply a manifestation of the one God. It is clear from the accounts in the Gospels that he constantly proclaimed a command of the God whom he tenderly invoked by the name of Father, the God to whom he completely entrusted his whole life. If we think of Jesus as God yet forget that he is a Son to God, then we understand nothing of him. Above all we fail to understand the meaning of his death on the cross. Having dedicated his whole life to the service of others, as his Father commanded, he also needed to confront martyrdom and offer his life to his Father in its entirety. And his Father raised him to life again, so that he could become our Way. All who commit themselves to follow him can make their lives into a gift, and so return to their Father. This is why the Church feels caught up in some design far greater than itself, part of a powerful movement which begins with the Father and returns to him. Knowing Jesus and speaking with him is like finding a trace of this design of the Father's, an indication of that great hope which is the Kingdom of God.

It is well known in the Church that our living involvement with an incomprehensible mystery so much greater than ourselves, certainly does not come from us. Jesus is not living today because we have brought him back to life. Not only that but neither would it be within our own power alone even to believe that he has risen. If we believe, then it is the work of grace, because our spirit has been transformed and remodelled by the Holy Spirit so that we may believe. This is why Jesus said, in the Gospel according to St John, chapter 16, that it is good for us that he should go away. We should not hold him before our eyes as just a good brother. By going away he sent us the Holy Spirit. The Spirit, penetrating deep within our hearts, gives us eyes to see in Jesus that which no human eye would be able to discern, namely that he is indeed the Son of God, always living, the one who saves us from sin and death.

In its awareness of faith therefore the Church feels like someone brought forth by the Holy Spirit. The Church gathers around Christ who lives in the heart of the believing community, so that the Church may be present in the world as a sign of its destiny, as a sign of that abundance of life which the world both can, and needs to, find by returning to the Father. When the Church wants to show its distinguishing characteristic, it makes the sign of the cross, in the name of the Father and of the Son and of the Holy Spirit. This is lest we forget that the Church's great discovery is the love of the risen and crucified One.

For those outside: a fact to keep in mind

Given the extraordinary nature of the facts, one might think that the Church has nothing of interest to say to a world which does not share that faith. Yet this is not the case. In the first place, those who gather within the Church have no intention of isolating themselves from the world. Christians continue to work, study, marry and struggle with life like everyone else, and with everyone else. Like everyone else, they do this in order to take up their responsibilities for the economic, social and political problems of the nation. In fact, they maintain that their faith in Christ gives their task in society a new motive and a fresh inspiration. Indeed, the news about Jesus is not simply a finished piece of history which, however interesting, is over and done with. It is the communication of an experience by which the Church lives in today's world like a sign of great hope. Those who are not in the Church still find the Church intermingling with their lives, so that they cannot always discern the Christian identity of those beside them. There are interesting and true stories told of worker priests who worked in a factory without their companions knowing them as priests. In fact this was necessary so that they might be recognised before all else as companions and brothers who could be trusted because they loved.

Naturally, there are also times, and aspects of the Church, which separate her from the world. Faith in the risen Christ leads to many things which the world finds meaningless: prayer, trust in God, the Christian understanding of suffering and death. The proclamation that Jesus is the only Saviour has brought the Church into conflict with all the other – with the innumerable other – pretended 'saviours' of the world. Although every human proposal can be worthy of the confidence of the Church, yet no human ideal can claim that depth and totality of commitment which is part of faith. Christians commit their conscience and their destiny to Jesus Christ and to him alone.

Chapter four

The things we want

The reality of the Church comes into being every time two or more people, by a free choice of faith, live out their experience of the risen Jesus. In this sense, the Church is always new and, in a certain way, elusive. However, in concrete reality, the Church acquires a certain corporeality: it gathers the necessary means, assumes stable forms, articulates itself within definite structures – in short, acquires all those aspects of a solid institution which we know so well.

We know certain things about this Church which is always under our noses. There are the churches, meaning by this those religious buildings in which the rites are enacted day by day. Within the actual religious building, or in adjacent buildings, there may well be a complex of rooms and other areas where catechumens and children are instructed and where initiatives are made towards the formation of young people. There various activities take place designed to help the poor, to give moral support to families, to be centres of collaboration and stimulus in social and political life.

Then, the Church has a whole load-bearing structure for carrying its major responsibilities. This is composed of priests and bishops and, at the top, the Pope with his apparatus of government. There are seminaries to train priests. In monasteries and convents live Christians who, by their vows of poverty, chastity and obedience, are dedicated to God and the service of their neighbour in a particular way; and this list could be greatly extended.

You might ask: is all this necessary? What is the principle on which all these component parts of the Church rest? Is it possible to isolate one element from which all the rest draw meaning, and without which all the rest would have no meaning?

The news

The first principle of the Church was the fact of one person communicating faith to another who then joins them in believing. It is this simple fact which gives life and vitality to the Church. This event, the living seed out of which the whole ecclesial system develops, is not something given once and for all. The Church only exists in so far as this communication of the news about Jesus' resurrection continues to be passed from one to the other.

This is why we can say that the basis of the Church is not institutional at all. It is in the mission, it is in 'being sent'. The Church only exists in so far as it is continually regenerated and reconstituted around this fundamental missionary activity.

The most important piece of news is that Jesus is risen. This proclamation, however, is part of a whole account telling who he was, what he said and did, how and why he died. None of those who proclaim the faith today have seen the risen Jesus for themselves, nor have they known him in the flesh. There are mystics and saints who say that they have contemplated him in a vision, but the faith of the Church is not based on the visions of saints. Those who say that Jesus is risen, and who recount the story, are transmitting news which they have received from others and have themselves believed. These others, in their turn, have learned it from yet others. The word of faith today, then, is a link in a chain stretching right back through the whole of Christianity. At the beginning of the chain stand the apostles, those who saw him with their own eyes and touched him with their hands, as St John says in the opening words of his first letter. The Christ they tell us about was no shade or phantom seen in a vision. The apostles ate with him even after the resurrection.

The apostles saw him, but they also did more than that. They believed in the mystery which he bore within himself. For this reason, their account is not something to be documented, like the siege of Carthage or the battle of Waterloo. On the other hand, neither is it simply a subjective experience, like that of some visionaries.

The Gospel is news; news which stands at the heart of the great history of faith. For believers, its truth is beyond doubt – believers gamble their lives on it. But its credibility does not rest upon documents in an archive, but on the seriousness and the human courage with which the experience of believers is given to the world. When I speak about my faith, I know that it is true even though I am not a good Christian, but I also know that no one can take it seriously if they cannot pass positive judgement on my own story. It is true that Christianity is founded only on Jesus and the witness of his apostles, but its martyrs and its poor, its ascetics and its heroes are also indispensable. It needs St Sebastian and St Francis, St Benedict and St Thomas More, Don Bosco, Pope John and Mother Teresa of Calcutta, the monks of Taizé and Helder Camara. The good news about Jesus is true because the Father has truly raised him from the dead, and the Holy Spirit has given me strength to believe it. All this can be transmitted to the world as a historical event because his apostles saw him. They saw his empty tomb and they met with him, risen from the dead. The proclamation, however, is only credible to the world in so far as it gives those who hope in it more life than people generally have.

The people

No matter how much we want to, we cannot communicate a faith which we do not share. Imagine a professor of Christian history, competent but a non-believer, and compare him or her with someone unlettered, who has never taken the Bible in his or her hands, but yet believes. The first will give you thorough information about the faith, but will not give you faith. The Church will never be born from his or her news about Jesus. The second might give you a very summary account of Christ: but, if you wish it, will share his or her faith with you and from your meeting will be born the Church.

So, of necessity, the Church is made up of the personal and original contribution of each believer, not from the simple objective transmission of a doctrine. There will be those who express their faith above all by gestures of prayer, who love tradition and pilgrimages, lighting candles and making novenas to the saints. Others, for their part, feel themselves called primarily to realise the mission of the Church through some work which daily puts them at the service of their neighbour; this is especially true for certain professions, such as medicine and teaching. Some express their Christianity in social services and politics; they may not seem particularly devout, but they give serious expression to Christ in the life of the world. Then again, there are people who have a life of faith which lacks outward expression, but which is a life of love, patience and generosity in family life, a life of strength in suffering lived in their everyday life.

Some, like priests and missionaries, put themselves at the service of the Church through a direct preaching of the Gospel or through pastoral care of the Christian community. Others make the search for God the primary occupation of their lives and enclose themselves in monasteries to pursue it. Some find the presence of Christ in dedication to the old, the poor, children or the sick. Others adopt or foster children who have no families. There are those who realise their Christian calling by contributing to the internal life of the community by such things as administration, catechism, education, recreation, liturgy and so on. Then there is no lack of those who give good service to the faith through their study; there is always a dialogue going on, aimed at understanding our shared human living, and the experience of faith can and should take part in this dialogue. So the list of the various ways of contributing to the Church can be infinitely extended.

The rationale behind this variety is very simple. Because faith is a free act and a personal choice, there can be no act of faith which is not stamped with the particular attributes of the one who makes it. The Holy

Spirit does not impose faith on us from outside but stirs it up in our hearts. If faith were a gift, in the sense of simply receiving a teaching from another, then it would be exactly the same for everyone. Instead of that, faith is the action of the Spirit within us, and so the gift of faith is always new, always distinct.

Those who are scandalised because the Church evolves, or amazed when they see an essential difference between Christians and communities of other traditions, have a sad picture of the Church and a moribund idea of faith. For them, faith is nothing but a list of formulae to be repeated and the Church nothing but the sacred bureaucracy designed to protect those formulae. According to them, Jesus has only preached one thing, and established certain norms in order to maintain it. Risen from the dead or not, there is very little that he has changed. What he has done is to consign this patrimony to the Pope to keep through the centuries and to impose on believers. Priests and bishops are simple functionaries whose task is to take the papal orders to the grass roots, and to celebrate prescribed rituals. They expect the faithful to obey, to pray and to live honestly.

In such a Church, self-knowledge would not be needed, nor would there be any serious possibility of mistakes, but neither would there be any likelihood of anything new. The great and desired advantage would be the security and the peace of a Christianity resting tranquilly in having nothing further to discover, nothing new to find, nothing to discuss, no differences to accept or confront. It is a strange way of thinking – imagining a God without dreams, a mummified Christ, a Spirit deprived of creativity, and all dedicated to the exclusive use of the ecclesiastical authorities – and utterly unable to be, as Jesus described it, like a wind which blows where it wills, of which we do not know whence it comes nor whither it goes. St Paul, indeed, speaks of the Church as a living body, of which the soul which gives it life is the Holy Spirit. This life flows through the members, each of which is wholly different from every other. Some are like hands, some eyes, some feet – each doing his or her own thing. Every Christian in the Church has his or her own life in this body which has only one soul, the Spirit, and one head, Christ. Within that, each has his or her own expression and particular function. There are thousands and thousands of different ways, called 'charisms' by Paul, gifts of the Spirit, by means of which each one lives their faith.

The book

The beauty of the situation we have just described is the Church's capacity to live in freedom, to give space to each one's personality, to immerse itself in various historical situations. The risk, of course, is that of not managing to be true to itself in the process.

Each person has his or her own way of seeing Jesus. There are many gifts of the Spirit and the experience of Christ is infinite, so the incredible richness of the life of humanity carried in the heart of God's mystery is never exhausted. The history of God was lived out, however, in the reality of flesh, in the womb of Mary, in the Nazareth workshop, in the streets and squares of Jerusalem, right up to the final shameful end upon the cross. It is Jesus who constructs the Church, not we who construct Jesus. It is a question of life and death to the Church that it preserve intact the memory of who Jesus really was in the history of humanity.

Jesus has left us no writings of his own but entrusted everything to the ears, the eyes and the love of those whom he called to live with him. Naturally, this was not by accident. If he had committed his message to writing, we would not need other people in order to know it – the document alone would be enough. Then there would never have been a Church. Now the Church must tell the world about a Christ who can be felt and seen in the Christians of today, in the concrete situations of today's world, but who is also the same original Christ as at the beginning.

This telling, like all transmission of faith, is based on the testimony of the apostles who saw him. They were the first witnesses. Because of this, they were also directly commissioned by Christ. It is enough to recall the passage in which Jesus changed the name of the apostle Simon to Peter, and thereby, through the witness of his faith, called him to be the foundational 'rock' of the Church. St Paul, passionate for freedom and the richness of charisms, invited his Christians to build their own kind of Church, but always on that same foundation. That foundation is the one laid by the apostles, the witnesses of Christ, given by him to the world once and for all.

If every experience of faith constitutes the Church, then the apostles' experience of Christ, and the history of faith lived by the apostolic Church, have an absolutely unique value. This fundamental witness is contained within the writings of the New Testament, made up of: the apostolic letters, the history of the apostles written by St Luke, the account of the visions of St John related in the Apocalypse and four accounts of the life of Jesus, known as 'the Gospels'. The Church has always considered these writings as a special gift from the Holy Spirit, and has made them its 'Canon' that is, its rule of faith. This sharing of the good news about Jesus runs all through the centuries, forming the Church in new and different ways. In the 'canonical writings' this sharing now has a way in which it can touch the original witness of Jesus' apostles. A book can be read and interpreted in many ways, but the fact that the book is there, saying the same words and being understood in the same way, means that there is one specific understanding of those words which is justified, and no other.

So we see how the written word becomes an instrument goading the Church to renewal. This may seem strange, but there it is. All the great reforming movements in the history of the Church have looked to the Gospel as their supreme tribunal of judgement for the Church. What would have been left of Christianity – after the corruptions of the papacy and the divisions of the Church, after the religious wars and the Inquisition, the philosophies, the heresies, the political compromises and the moral decadence – what would have been left, had the Church not held in its hands the disturbing power of these four slim books called 'the Gospels'?

The facts

If the communication of faith had been only through this or that person's personal experience, then numerous small groups of believers would have sprung up, itinerant movements around this or that religious phenomenon, rather as happens about someone who has had visions. But the Church is more than a simple communion based on emotion and feeling. Focused on a book, living a rule of faith contained in that book and with the task of bringing the apostolic message into being exactly as it has been received, the Church builds a true and genuine Christian community. At this point we see that each single Christian is not a solitary batsman, nor are Christians like hermits in contemplation or cavaliers who have wandered from the world's battlefields of faith. Nor are they a movement of opinion of a mystical character. The historical solidarity of their witness and the continuity of their communion bind them to a common life. In that common life, the shared works are a concrete, and historically verifiable, sign of that which is within.

The main thrust of a Christian community's programme of shared life is to bear witness to the faith. This is because the Church believes that Jesus is risen from the dead, and is also aware of him living among us, so its first specific task is to take this news to everyone, to tell everyone in the world about him. The second is a task of love. A communion of deep feeling, like the communion of faith, moves into action when we need each other. Because the Church is an open communion, founded on Jesus who gave his life for us all, the Christian community must make itself available to everyone in love for all. It is the task of the Church to discover the needs of people around it, to specify the places of pain and to bring them a sign of God's love through works of community. In its own area, the Christian community must become a trusted point of reference for all those who need support. The openness of the community should tolerate no discrimination. Anyone who has once received with faith the words of Christ about his commandment of love self-destructs the moment he or she close his or her heart to anyone else.

The third purpose of the Church's programme of

life comes from its hope of salvation. Certainty in God, in the risen Jesus, offers the world a future. It also obliges the Christian community to share in the world's journey towards a better future for all. This means that we must involve ourselves in cultural, social and political movements. We must bear the burdens and the risks alongside others, collaborating or challenging as may be the case, but always intertwining the Christian road with that of the world. For this world, in spite of mistakes and falls, risk and daring, second thoughts and leaps forward, struggles to create a better life and a more just society. If the Church has the kingdom of God to announce, it will not be done by gazing out of the window, waiting for the end when God will impose his justice.

The rituals

The normal place for the Church to live out its experience of faith is in daily life. The mystery of Jesus who is alive, of the Spirit who gives life and of the Father to whom all things tend, comes into our history, is realised first and foremost in the facts of daily life. This is why we can dare to say that the Church is a sort of great and continuous 'sacrament'. In fact, just as baptism and confirmation and the other seven sacraments of God give God's grace to those who come to them, so – through the very fact that the Church exists – God is working mysteriously for the salvation of us all.

However, regarding this sacramental aspect of the Church's life, we must point out that the seven sacramental rituals each offer a different reality. They are by no means ordinary actions of everyday life; they are symbolic gestures, traditional and very ancient, which are placed in a particular climate of prayer and are being enacted in places which are normally apart from the ordinary activities of the world. There the Christian community can express itself poetically, in music and song, in an appropriate architectural ambience and in a beautiful ritual. Liturgy is a world unto itself, having no meaning or content to the unbeliever. It is a world which only interests the unbeliever as a subject of historical curiosity or artistic expression.

For the Church, though, what meaning is there to be drawn from the celebration of liturgical rites? First of all, to perform an action focused on God, has the effect of testing the world, simply because it has no meaning for the world. It obliges the world to question itself about the ultimate meaning of life; it does not allow the world to forget the question of God. Non-believers are shocked when Christians 'waste time' in prayer. Monks and nuns who are dedicated to contemplation are seen as a nonsense; but it is precisely through this time, 'wasted' in singing God's praises and fulfilling the rituals of worship, that the Church gains an accurate awareness of its new task in history. The daily works of the Christian community must be done with maximum efficiency; the Church bears witness to the faith and hopes that others will also come to believe; it puts into effect works of charity and co-ordinates the works of its members, and it shares in the world's own undertakings with the aim of creating a better society. However, the effectiveness of its programmes is not the deepest hope of the Church. Many battles can be lost because the war is won. Every single Church enterprise may fail, but the salvation of everyone is already assured by the resurrection of Christ. So when the Christian 'takes a rest', 'wastes time', 'sings God's praises' the Church is taking every task back to the source of greatest hope – the risen Jesus.

In fact, the liturgy of the Church is essentially a recalling of the facts of Christ's life, whether through reading, the repetition of gestures or the creation of evocative symbols. Look at what happens at Mass. First, the Bible is read, so that we can make judgements, and weigh the facts of the Church's life against those of Jesus. Then we repeat the scene of the Last Supper of Jesus – this is a reconstruction, almost a theatrical representation; we eat that bread and drink that chalice, just as the apostles did. Because he is alive in the Church and his Spirit gives life to the gathered community, the repetition of his words becomes a genuine mystery of a true communion with his body, which is sacrificed for the good of us all. At this point, the Church's action reaches maximum effectiveness. The Church renews the one gesture which is unfailingly effective for the salvation of the world, that is, the sacrifice of Christ. The Church draws upon that hope in the light of which the Church itself can afford to be compromised in the eyes of human hopes because she holds this certainty, that beyond all human failure the Crucified One is risen and waiting.

The priests

The Church has a vital need to be concentrated within mystery in order to be spread abroad in life. Obviously, a Church which did nothing but create liturgies would make no sense. Salvation comes from God, but lives in ordinary life. At the same time, though, a Church which abandoned all liturgy would not make sense either. It would be an instrument of a purely human programme of salvation, its hope would die within the confines of the more or less relevant historical efficiency of its works.

No one denies that a Christian community, like every other form of social grouping, must be organised and must have people in responsibility. Today, authority in the Church, as in the rest of society, is in the firing line. At one end of the scale are those who, a bit harshly, blame their loss of faith on a meeting with an inadequate priest. At the other end lie the great theological problems of the churches of the reformation who for centuries have rejected the Catholic imposition of an ecclesiastical hierarchy. Pope and bishops are frequently criticized, they are often accused of foolishly wanting to push themselves into political questions, or authoritatively imposing a morality which is inadequate for our times.

A priest is more likely to enjoy a vague general esteem, or approval, for social work, help to the homeless, rehabilitation of drug addicts – rather than approval for his faith in God and in the Christ whom he professes and preaches.

In addition, there are those who, in the light of all that we have said so far about the Church, declare that they have no need of leaders, laws or hierarchies. The Holy Spirit moves them from within their hearts, and they do not see why an external guide or a superior authority is necessary. St Paul stated quite clearly that there is one mediator between God and human beings, Jesus Christ, who gave his life that we might know the Father. To think that the ordinary person should run to a priest and his sacred power in order to approach God seems an idea more pagan than Christian. It seems like a return to witchcraft, the death of all enthusiasm and liberty in faith.

The presence of priests and bishops in the early days of the Church is well attested in the New Testament, in few but precious passages. The apostolic Church did not want to institute a new priesthood which would supersede the Jewish one. We have one priest, Jesus himself: this was the decisive and important affirmation of the apostolic faith. Jesus is our mediator with God, and he became so not through a cultic celebration which already existed but through serving his Father and his brethren even to the supreme sacrifice on the cross. This is all, it is enough. If we read the letter to the Hebrews, we see that the whole burden of the discourse rests on this conviction. In the very early days, the Christian communities, which were scattered here and there around the Mediterranean basin, had no need of much organisation. The apostles and their first collaborators travelled a great deal and kept in touch through letters. Their authority derived quite spontaneously from their prestige. When their role was contested, as happened to St Paul, their defence rested on the fact that it was Christ himself who had commanded them, and the whole faith of the Church leant on their witness.

When the apostles began to vanish from the scene, there was a problem: how to guarantee continuity of faith for the Church? The first thought was a written document; but the faith was a rich and vital experience that could not be contained in words, any more than it could be expressed in a list of doctrines and moral precepts. There had to be another solution. Chapter 20 of the Acts of the Apostles tells us about it, in the context of a very interesting episode. The apostle Paul found himself at Miletus on the west coast of present-day Turkey, travelling towards Palestine, and those in charge of the Christian community in the nearby city of Ephesus had come to see him. In Greek they were called the 'presbuteroi' which means the 'elders' – not in years but elders in responsibility. In fact, in the early days of the Church, it seems that there was nobody truly and properly responsible beyond the apostles, but during the last years of the apostolic era these groups of 'presbyters' emerged. They were also called *episkopoi*, meaning: those who keep watch, guardians, the leaders of the community.

In this meeting at Miletus the apostle gave a sort of testimony. He recalled that this journey to Jerusalem would be his last and that he was ready for imprisonment and martyrdom there. Therefore, with great emotion on all sides, he spelt out how much he had done and suffered for the communities themselves. Above all, he wanted them never to forget what Jesus had done for the Church, bringing it to birth and achieving its very existence through his blood on the cross. Paul was preoccupied with the future. He feared the 'ravening wolves' which were ready to scatter the flock of sheep. This image of wolves is Jesus' own, from the Gospel of Matthew, where it means 'false prophets', that is, those who pretend to bring the word of God but in reality deform it. The inheritance of the apostles, who had actually seen the Lord and touched him with their own hands, was not to be lost. Paul recommends to the presbyters that they keep watch over the Church as good and watchful shepherds, since none other than the Holy Spirit had destined them for this task. They had been invested for their mission by the gesture of laying hands upon them, a gesture which asks for and grants a particular charism of the Spirit.

This original structure of presbyters, also called bishops, who were collegially responsible for the community, rapidly developed and expressed itself in various ways. At the beginning of the second century, as we see from the letters of Ignatius, Bishop of Antioch, every church had a bishop responsible for it, and he was helped by a council of priests, while the deacons' service was still not clearly defined. We are talking here about urban communities who were small in number and who gathered together to celebrate under the presidency of the bishop. He was the one responsible for the unity of the church in the one faith, offering the one Eucharist for them all. It seems that without a bishop, the church did not really find itself, did not feel guaranteed in its faith. For this reason, right from the start, a church without a bishop did not celebrate the Eucharist. Later on, when the number of Christians had grown and the Church had spread out into the surrounding countryside, individual priests were authorised to guide the communities springing up in the villages and they were also placed at the head of the various communities of the Church coming into being within the cities. So, little by little, the collegial organisation of priests developed and gradually loosened the bond, that had originally been so close, between the faithful and the bishop. In time, it was the priest who was the true pastor of the community and the bishop became a part of the wider catholic Church. This was even more so as the development of the papacy gave the Church a structure like that of the empire. The bishop became dependent on the Pope and was more involved in the government of the universal Church. Meanwhile, deacons gradually vanished from the scene altogether and only reappeared with the last Council, Vatican II.

Today, the normal Christian community has a priest for its pastor. He became a priest by receiving a particular sacrament called that of Sacred Orders. He was consecrated by a bishop who had seen that the Holy Spirit has given him the gifts and attitudes which would form him into a good shepherd in the Church. Through this sacrament, those spontaneous gifts of the Spirit become the grace to fulfil this task and also a consecration for it, a task which the whole Church is then called upon to acknowledge. The priest should be the first to communicate the faith to others. Like everyone else, he does this by sharing his own personal experience of Christ. Through his charism as shepherd, he bears witness above all to the Christ who preaches, and in this way he preserves the continuity and apostolic authenticity of the faith. Through the rich interweaving of all these various ways of feeling and sharing the faith, his testimony acts as a necessary focal point around which the unity of the Church can be built, a unity which always roots itself in the apostolic faith of its beginnings.

The apostle Paul wrote to the Christians at Corinth: 'Though you have countless guides in Christ, you do not have many fathers. For I became your father in Christ Jesus through the gospel' (1 Cor 4:15). Every priest can say these words to his community if, like the apostle, he has paid the price of his fatherhood by involvement, weariness and suffering. It is from this basic role that a priest derives his pastoral responsibility and also his authority within the community. The one who begets is also responsible for growth and education. This is why the priest's own witness to his faith binds him so strongly to his community and urges him to work so tirelessly for its growth in faith. When diversification generates so much tension that the authenticity of the faith and the basic unity of the community at greater risk than can be dealt with by ordinary pastoral methods, then the pastor must exercise his authority and each Christian his or her task of obedience.

Finally, what is the task of the priest when the community gathers to celebrate the liturgy and to seek a sacramental and ritual expression for its daily experience of Christ? Our minds turn to the Eucharist. The community gathers in order to re-enact the scene of Christ's Last Supper. The believers, like the apostles, gather around a table on which they have placed bread and wine. Then they need to find one who will take the part of Christ and, at the head of the table, break the bread for them, one who will share the chalice with them in Christ's name. Who should this be? It could be one chosen by chance, or it could be the holiest, or the one who has best been able to bear witness to the Gospel before the world. Or it could be he who, by reason of a sacrament, represents that necessary link which binds the community to the apostles' witness to Christ. The Eucharist is not simply a representation of Jesus' Last Supper, but the mystery of his true presence at work in the Church. The priest mediates Jesus' role in his own local church, through the mystery of grace which the priest carries within himself because of his consecration, and also by the unique rapport he has with his community.

In the light of the gifts and competence of a priest in his community, it seems clear that his responsibility has meaning only if the Church is living and active in its members. In fact, if the Church were not so constructed as to have a plurality of charisms, there would be no need for any unifying function. If the apostolic message were not being handed on in new ways, unique and original to the occasion, we would not need any guarantee of continuity. Only that which lives in diversity can be brought into unity. Only that which is always breaking new ground needs to be held in oneness. We only authenticate the continually creative; we only co-ordinate the varied; we only share the table with Christ if those around the table are the apostles.

Chapter five

The shape of the Church

The Church, in its basic structure, is just as Jesus planned and wished. It is founded on a faith which we all share by baptism. Its mission is to carry the Gospel of salvation to everybody. It is enriched with some indispensable means, such as Holy Scripture, the ministry of its priests and bishops and so on.

In fact, though, the Church across the centuries has presented itself to the world in a great many different ways. The external garment which it wears at any given time is partly determined by the circumstances in which it finds itself living. For example, our own time has seen a notable turning point, for the great inner struggle of the Church today seems to be, at root, a difficult transition from having the structures of a society to having those of a community. It is important that we understand what is happening, lest, in the process of change, the Church were to lose its loveliest and most precious characteristics, that of being what the Bible and Christian tradition both call the people of God.

From about the fourth century, when the Roman Empire adopted Christianity as its official religion, until the fifteenth century, with the so-called 'discovery' of America, Christians were convinced that the world was entirely Christian. It was known that there were people of other religions, or none, but these were understood as pockets of resistance to the preaching of the Gospel, and they had to be kept under control or eliminated. The boundaries of the Church appeared to coincide with those of the civil structures of the known world.

In the fifteenth century, at the high point of this impressive historical experience, the Council of Florence could proclaim that 'there is no salvation outside the Church', and in those circumstances such a statement was quite logical. 'Outside the Church' were only those who obstinately refused to be inside. By that very choice, they automatically chose to remain outside and in opposition to the very group within which God had placed faith, the sacraments and all the means of salvation. So the Church took the form of a civil society, with the same social and political structures. It was governed by the State in temporal matters and by the ecclesiastical hierarchy in all that concerned the soul and eternal salvation.

By the start of our own era, this kind of world had already begun to break up. Nationalist States arose from the ashes of the empire, and the Church was tragically divided within itself by the Reformation and the birth of the Protestant Churches. However, Catholicism continued to focus on the vision it had received from the ancient and medieval worlds, as on a picture of the ideal way for the Church to site itself in history. This mentality is very deeply rooted, and can still find expression, even in today's pluralistic society. Some people cannot recognise that the situation has changed.

It is quite clear, however, that the old, compact, unitary world, with a Catholic faith shared by everyone, has completely gone. Not only that, but the modern political ideal (exalted and desired, even if rarely put into practice) is of a democratic society, which welcomes and respects everyone, of whatever faith, customs and world view. A society inspired by such a political ideal will base its government on the consent of the majority rather than on any religious or ideological principles.

There is, obviously, a separation between the Church and the secular State. And yet, to abundant – andjustified – criticism, the Church has, in its time, organised itself along the lines of the State with its own bureaucracy and structures of power. It has often been said that in this way the Church tends to base itself on law rather than on faith and love of neighbour. The results of such a deformation are obvious in some of our parishes. There the Christian is completely lost in the anonymity of belonging to a Church which is almost automatic, more like an office than something freely chosen and personally life-giving, where the priests administer the sacraments like employees in an office compiling certificates of residence.

A vision of such a Church formed along the models of 'society' has today fallen into desuetude, to say the very least.

The great strength of the Catholic Church after the second Vatican Council lay in its search for new ways of being and new ways of participating in civil society. The magic word for this search, a word heard on all sides, was 'community'. What was wanted was to overcome the anonymity of belonging to the Church. If I am baptised, then I am a member of the parish in which I live. Yet it is certainly not the fact of being inscribed in the register that makes me a sharer in the family of the faith, for that is a family in which the faithful live out their communion in Christ.

Today, far more keenly than before, a need is felt for an everyday experience of real rapport between people. Often, indeed, the community is gathered around the priest, it has a defined territory and is often blessed with a central focus of activity which is, more often than not, very well organized. There will be homes, centres of worship, meeting rooms, youth clubs, schools and works of mercy. Yet such a parish can fail to meet this need that people feel, simply because it is too big, the people too disparate and everything too bureaucratic.

Small groups, on the other hand, which spring up spontaneously and are not at all organised or localized, can draw together people who are much of an age, or are temperamentally alike, or from the same social background. Then it is much easier for them to communicate and live, with intensity and enthusiasm, that experience of exchange between various ways of knowing Christ; and it is this experience which is both the raw material from which the Church is built and the place where it happens. When such a group gathers informally to celebrate the Eucharist, it is easy to generate a loving atmosphere. Community and communion with Jesus become a felt reality, something one can almost reach out and touch. People then come away from Mass with joy, with a spiritual recharge which is not easily lost. They compare it with Mass celebrated in some public place where the people gather anonymously, unable to mean their 'Amen' or rejoice in the 'Alleluia'; where, at the end of Mass, they leave without anyone even sharing a greeting. The contrast is so sharp that we must acknowledge the first to be a true experience of Church and the second not. In some city churches, particularly, there is sometimes an atmosphere of such cold anonymity that the churches seem more like places of business than centres of religious ceremonial.

For all these reasons, parishes have given priority to seeking new forms of community, forms where there is some personal communication between individuals and therefore a chance of having some experience of a shared life. Where parishes have proved too big, small communities have been formed in the huge tower blocks or in areas of a particular nature and character. It then becomes possible to preach the Gospel to new people who are far from the faith, simply because there is some interpersonal rapport. In the cities, especially, the presence of small Christian communities among the different groupings of people is indispensable, if we wish to invite those who do not believe to know and live an experience of faith.

For many, however, it seems that the parish is not enough and that it no longer meets their needs. Then people look elsewhere for nourishment and for ways to share their faith. This is why the Catholic world today vibrates with myriad groups, associations and movements. They offer a form of Christian life which is strongly bound to a particular group. This, in its turn, is acceptable because it gathers together people who, in one way or another, know each other and have some affinity with each other. We are talking here about those who belong to a particular social class or who live near each other – as happens, for instance, with some kinds of association and with some groups of young people. That community is then marked by a particular spirituality. This might happen in a group which is linked to some religious order or in the neo-catechumenate.

In other cases, a strong community bond is forged by people's dedication to a specific task within the wider mission of the Church. Sometimes the determining and distinguishing factor of a community is rather hard to define. It might just be the language or a certain style, revealed by the way they pray, meet and function. Such a community will nearly always focus around a person of considerable spiritual stature who either begot the group or inspired it in some way. Sometimes the community shows hardly any interest in the socio-political aspects of the Church's mission. Each member decides for him or herself how he or she will fulfil his or her civil responsibilities. Others again, are very conscious of their civil duties and see themselves as far more effective when there is a strong community bond by which they can exert their influence on the Church and society.

The widely varied forms of community found in the Church today certainly offer many people the chance of a strong ecclesial experience. In addition to the basic Christian communities which are part of the actual parish structure, we should take note of an important characteristic common to most of these associations, groups and movements. It is this: that they not only try to share the basic faith of the Gospel of Jesus, but also a particular spiritual approach, or a specific charism, or a different way of living in society. Or else they have a single interest which they pursue or, simply, a certain style of life. In this resides their strength and their limitation.

People

Right from the earliest times, the Church has been keenly aware of the power of community bonds. In the Acts of the Apostles, Luke often bears witness to this:

And all who believed were together and had all things in common; and they sold their possessions and goods and distributed them to all, as any had need. And day by day, attending the temple together and breaking bread in their homes, they partook of food with glad and generous hearts, praising God and having favour with all the people. And the Lord added to their number day by day those who were being saved (Acts 2:44-47).

It is very interesting to see that the first generation Christians had no thought of creating a new religion, but instead took their place among the people of Israel and in their own great tradition of faith. In the text quoted above, we read how the Christians went to the Temple together with the other Jews. St Paul, without any scruple, called the Church the 'Israel of God' (Gal 6:16). It is true that the majority of Jews did not recognise Jesus as the Messiah, but those who did never considered themselves a movement or sect within Judaism, but rather as the fulfilment, the final form of the people called by God. Serious problems began to arise when the pagans came to faith in Jesus. These were only resolved, after much tension and long debate when they all realized that Jesus had superseded the Mosaic law; the law was no longer the absolutely necessary instrument of salvation. However, this was never meant to be an exodus from the great hive of their people's history. In Jesus, their ancient hopes had found fulfilment and a basis for unity. They were no longer bound together by a shared law and a shared nationality, for he had broken these ancient limits. He had gathered to himself a people formed from every race on earth.

The great battles of St Paul against those who wanted to contain salvation within the ancient law of Israel were a ferocious defence of a fundamental principle: in order to belong to the people of God and be saved, all that is needed is faith in Jesus. Arising from this fundamental principle, the Church redefined itself as the 'people'. Hebrews and Greeks, men and women, slave and free, were all part of it, and even children were very quickly included in the Church – new born babies were baptised in the name of their parents' faith and the faith of the community. Nor were the lukewarm, the doubting and the sinners excluded. Popes and bishops knew very well that in the latter case, to begin with, quite a few of them would have to be excluded from the Church and the Church's story. In fact, once someone had been baptised, they could never be expelled from the Christian community in any categorical and formal manner. Excommunication is a deprivation of the right to receive the sacraments, rather than expulsion from the Church. It is imposed on those who, in all essentials, want to continue as members of the community even though they have attacked the teaching of the faith or publicly behaved viciously in contrast to the Gospel morality or the Church's rules for living together.

This form of being a people was perpetuated in the Church by, above all, the baptism of babies. As a way of drawing people to itself, it inserted the Church very powerfully into history, into culture and the traditions of the people. The Church is 'the people of God', not some spiritual aristocracy which is distant from the ordinary human way of living. This is why some people feel they have been deceived when they look at the life of a normal Christian community. They expect to find spiritual *Supermen* and *Superwomen* and instead meet poor people, burdened with incoherence and weakness. On the other hand, this very fact enables others to join the Church looking for salvation, people who are sinners, those at whom others point the finger, but people who are loved and sought out by Jesus. Such people understand how the hope of humanity is a response to God's grace, rather than something which we have earned or deserved.

Chapter six

The supporting structures

Very slowly the Gospel, the good news of Jesus, spread. Like yeast, it entered hearts and fermented, raising the dough of human existence and bringing forth saving fruit of every kind. At the same time, the Church extended its boundaries and increased. This whole process is simply the vigorous movement of Tradition, though we are not using the word here in its more ordinary sense. There are many minor Christian traditions, such as the blessing of the house, or a procession for the feast of a patronal saint. These are not what we have in mind. Tradition, written with a capital 'T', means the passing from one person to another, one people to another, one generation to another, of belief in Jesus. The Church is born from and lives by this impressive movement of Tradition. Its first fruit, in fact, is the coming together of the Christian community which, in its turn, accepts Tradition's responsibility for all those whom the Christians meet, and for all future generations.

What sort of community comes from Tradition and takes on this responsibility for others? The sort of community which forms around the Gospel message and rests upon its faith in Christ. No one should forget that the Church is, basically, a people. The community is Church only in so far as it is rooted in people. From this, and from the need to guarantee the preservation of true Tradition, come the Church's fundamental structures. These are the sort of thing every community must have, at least to some extent, as points of reference.

The parish

A bell tower, a church, a so-called 'holy house', a complexus, rich or poor as the case may be, a meeting place, catechism and various other activities and the constant presence of the priest as well as some helpers for religious services and all the many necessary tasks – these are part of the panorama of the parish in our section of the town and our part of the country.

Is this the whole of what the Church is?

Obviously not. However, it is true that in practice the parish is the first point of reference. The parish is the most immediate face of the Church, the one which defines its community basis. In reality, though, the Church exists wherever a single believer is found going about his or her daily business. The Church is present wherever Christians gather, whether to pray or to organise themselves in working for their mission in the world. They are seen as the people of God only when, gathered together in faith and taking their place in the community, they make no demands on each other beyond those of the pure and simple profession of their Catholic faith. This is the meaning of parish.

A person is a member of a certain parish community simply by reason of sharing this faith and living in that area. The territorial criterion allows the creation of a community of people. In fact, this comes solely from sharing the faith, not from any grouping of believers for some particular reason, nor from their being selected on the basis of a characteristic vocation; these are not what form community.

Only when the Church is primarily composed of communities of this kind is every believer's right to belong guaranteed. Otherwise, a believer can be required to share more than the faith, to adopt a certain style of life, or a particular charism, or the goal of some specific objective. A parish has many defects, much denounced these days, but it has this one great advantage: it is a Church open to everyone, it is a gathering in which the faithful come together with no distinctions of age, social status, affinity of taste or culture. The Church takes shape perfectly only when it is a community of everyone, when everyone is there expressing their unity to the full in their celebration of the Mass. The real place for the Eucharist is in a big church which has room for the old and for the babies, for professors and illiterate, where the preaching is in the language of the farmers and workers, and songs are sung which are loved by every housewife. The elite groups of young intellectuals, Christian enthusiasts, mystics or politically active Catholics, all need to keep sending the roots of their Church experience down into ordinary soil, to weave it into the wide and varied fabric of the people. The Word of God is found in the teaching Jesus gave to fishermen. The *Gloria* was sung at his birth to shepherds, the Eucharist was simply made with bread and wine. Jesus did not reveal himself as the prize and consolation of the just, but as the friend of sinners. This is why the Church cannot shut itself away in a 'holy huddle' or give up celebrating the Eucharist with the church doors open to the High Street. Those who would come in are not only enthusiasts for the faith, or the politically and culturally privileged, but people who are weary of life, people who doubt and are unsure, inarticulate Christians and superstitious ones, the uninstructed and the mentally handicapped. The Church is God's table for the poor.

The priest who takes care of this kind of Church will be an ordinary priest. Usually, he will be neither a Franciscan nor a Dominican nor a Jesuit. He has a vow of celibacy because he has committed himself to his community, but otherwise he will live an ordinary life like every other Christian. The basic reason why he is there is to maintain the people of God in the unity of genuine faith, the faith which the apostles announced to the world. In this sense, the priest is at the service of all the Christians in his area, even if these also belong to some more specifically defined group as well. And he is at the service of the entire population whom he finds in his parish, because the Church is there for them, not for itself.

The diocese

Such a Church is probably not particularly efficient on the social, cultural and political levels. Its witness of faith may seem weak and ill-equipped to catch the world's attention. In compensation, however, it can be a true companion on the journey for people, for the whole crowd of human beings as they travel together, a companion for all those who seek the way to the kingdom of God in the humble and the ordinary, even for those who seek the kingdom without knowing that they do so.

If a man of today, here among us, seeks the Church, it is obvious that he will first meet up with the parish. However, if we want to seek the Church in its historical development, we will meet it primarily in another of its fundamental structures: the diocese. Primitive Christianity first evolved in the cities. The form which those first Christian communities assumed was quite adequate for the urban context. In the first centuries, there were not many Christians and they used to form one gathering in order to celebrate their one Eucharist around the bishop, who would have been surrounded by his priests and deacons. It was only later, when the urban communities had increased in number and Christianity had spread into the rural areas, that the Christian community took on the shape of the districts and villages. Then the priests became more scattered and a change took place in the understanding of the priesthood, that is in the old collegial system of collaboration with the bishop. Each priest became the pastor of a much smaller community. Within that community, he celebrated the Eucharist and Christians lived out the fullness of their ordinary Christian life.

This historical process explains why it is that the parish is not the Church in the full sense, even though it has its own sufficiently autonomous life. The priest, the one who guarantees that the Gospel is preached in its apostolic authenticity, is always sent for that purpose. The community does not consecrate its own priest, does not lay hands on him or delegate his powers to him, as it might for one deputed to Parliament or a trade union. Even if he had been born a Christian and had grown up in the parish, even if he has been chosen by his community, the priest is still someone sent, someone who comes from afar. Therefore, he is a messenger. Through the chain of the apostolic succession, a chain which is 2,000 years long, he bears with him a letter written by other men of another time, those who have seen with their own eyes and touched with their own hands. The delivery of this message is effected through a sacrament and is a gift of the Holy Spirit. So it is always the bishop who consecrates and sends a priest to be the pastor of a community.

The fact that a parish community has all the components for a full life of the Church but not the power to ordain itself a priest, and that its priest cannot create his successor by ordaining another priest, exercises a beneficial restraint because it opens the community to the universal dimension of the Church. The parish must seek the fullness of being Church in a wider context, it must look beyond the confines of its own territory, rooting the apostolic character of the parishioners' own faith somewhere beyond themselves. In his first letter to the Christians in Corinth (who were a bit proud and closed) St Paul wrote: 'Did the word of God originate with you, or are you the only ones it has reached?' (1 Cor 14:36). So it is in communion with the bishop and other communities that the parish community finds the true reality and the genuine dimensions of the Church.

So we begin to see that the ministry of the bishop has a true and unique catholic dimension. He is the pastor who is responsible for a group of communities called 'the diocese'. He is also a member of a universal organisation called the episcopal college, responsible for the whole of the Catholic Church. Thus, through the bishop, the community's place within the vast network of the Catholic communion is recognised. There are a number of consequences from this; for instance: the task laid upon the richer communities with regard to the poorer ones; the task of those who have matured in the faith towards those who are just beginning; the more equitable distribution of services and resources, of initiatives for the expansion of the faith and the founding of new churches; the constant interaction with all the different ways of living and communicating the experience of Christ. Finally, because the community has a link with the universal episcopate, it also has a voice with which to speak to the world, and this voice is all the stronger for being united and universal. Through it, the community is able to grasp those responsibilities it has for our journey through history.

Why 'Catholic'

We have seen how the communion which binds together those who share the faith, is like the breath of the Church reaching out to wider and wider horizons, how even in its most circumscribed and reduced form, the soul of the Church is 'catholic'.

'The Catholics' is a term used to distinguish Christians of our Church from those of the Protestant and Orthodox Churches. However reluctantly, Orthodox and Protestants reserve the term 'Catholic' for us but every Church must describe itself as catholic. This name is normally given to that Church which is in union with the Roman Pontiff, because he was there, bearing this title, before the divisions by which the other Churches became independent, often in very dramatic circumstances. In fact, for a Church to call itself 'catholic' simply means that it claims to be universal and world-wide, and the Church of Christ could be nothing else. To be catholic, however, does not necessarily mean that it must exist in every single country and on all continents, but rather that, even when very small, the church community bears the mystery of the universe within itself. This means that the Church can never feel itself bound only to one culture, one country, one social class, nation or people.

The catholic soul of the church is always committed to spreading an experience of the faith. This means not only testifying to Christ before everyone we meet and thus extending the community, but also demonstrating a kind of audacity, a tireless and constant sending of people throughout the world in order to carry the Gospel to new countries where no one as yet has heard of it. So Catholicism has this inner urgency to extend the boundaries of our communion. This urgency is alleviated by the wide network of connections through which the various churches scattered around the world are united so that in the end they make the one and only Church of Christ, a Catholic Church indeed. On the personal level, all this is takes on value when, in London, Switzerland or India, you find a church and, side by side with your brothers and sisters, partake of the same Body of Christ.

The catholic aspect of the Church is one of those things which turns up, however intangibly, in the ordinary life of the Christian community. People live the life of the Church in the simplicity of their everyday contacts, in charity and prayer together, in the attention they give to the small and the great problems of the nation and the district, in places of work or study. The catholic dimension is like an atmosphere, like the air; if you do not have it, then you feel you are dying. The Church would soon be reduced to a conventicle if it lacked this communication and these collaborative initiatives. The flow of its prayer would come to an end and it would quickly become defined by its internal difficulties, shut in with its own small problems. It would be incapable of sensing the greatness of Christ at the level of the world's problems. Then it would be enormously impoverished spiritually, the universal Christ reduced within it to a little idol kept for home use and consumption.

Bishops and Pope

If it is the bishop who first opens the door of the little village community or district onto the universal dimension of the Church, then the key of this catholic building is, in the end, the Pope. He is the Bishop of Rome. As such, he has a particular task in the Church, because it was in Rome that St Peter was killed and buried. Jesus entrusted Peter with the mission of being, by the witness of his faith, the ultimate foundation of the united structure, the basis for the Church's solidarity. The episode in which Peter bears witness is told in St Matthew's Gospel, chapter 16. When Jesus asked his disciples what they thought of him, Simon replied with a beautiful profession of faith, whereupon the Lord changed his name to Peter ('the Rock') and made this Rock the foundation stone of the Church.

The Pope is the centre of communion for all the bishops and for the whole Church. Each Christian community finds its own recognized place in the unity of the whole through its link with the bishop, and the bishop in his turn is a part of the college of bishops. This college of bishops, though, only has any existence and only functions as a college in so far as it includes the Pope. It is hard to find a politico-juridical parallel for this, because the Pope is not like some absolute monarch. The Church's shape and unity do not come from the Pope alone, but from the college of all the bishops. Nor is the Pope like a constitutional monarch, for the decisions taken by the bishops do not simply oblige the Pope to sign on the dotted line.

It is interesting to see what happens when the Pope summons an ecumenical council, that is, an assembly of all the bishops. As in all assemblies, there are complex and prolonged debates and lively theoretical clashes as well as a variety of opinions expressed. The bishops then work together towards a majority opinion so that they can arrive at a decision in line with the norms laid down for them. Unlike a parliament, the dominant party does not strive simply to gain its point, if necessary by only one vote; and, before all else, they make sure that the Pope is with them, or gives his consent. Then, over and above what the rules lay down, they need in some way to regroup the college of bishops within itself, so that the decision can, in the end, be the decision of all the bishops of the Catholic Church. To this end, the majority in a council will try, as far as possible, to incorporate the opinions of the minority, expressing them in the form of amendments. Afterwards, the decrees are signed by the Pope and all the bishops.

This system is hard to understand by the logic of parliamentary assemblies, or the juridical regulations of any civil collegial organisation. The business with numbers and ballot papers in an urn is a necessary instrument because this is how the voice of the assembly speaks. The statements which eventually turn up in the council's urn to be voted on are established by everyone listening to everyone else, and through the effort to perceive the value of every charism in the universal Church, for this is what the bishops are expressing. In this attempt at general listening, the opinion held by the Pope is indispensable, simply because his charism is to be the key of the whole thing, to give the final determining weight to catholic unity.

Obviously, this is a presupposition of faith. This conviction that the Holy Spirit gives life to the Church in all its expressions, and leads it to catholic unity through all its particular charisms, is a conviction which is heard and understood by each one according to his or her own specific role. Obviously, too, the Pope is not going to hurry to cast his vote or put forward his own view. He too will listen and consider, clarify and mediate, and draw diversity together into apostolic and catholic unity. The Pope does not do this only when a council meets; rather it is part of the daily exercise of his ministry, of his constant contact with the bishops and faithful from every community. He fulfils his task through a patient and unceasing weaving together of the relationships between the churches, churches which are so different from each other and yet each capable of showing a single face, the face of the Church of Christ.

The fullness of the Pope's roles and powers have varied greatly down the centuries. There have been times when the Pope, as sovereign of a powerful, rich and well-armed State, seemed more like a worldly leader, an absolute and undisputed ruler in the Church. At such times, the Church has been an extreme example of a society which, while wanting to be Christian, had subjected even its definitions of ideology and morality to the organisations of civil life. It was not so in the first centuries, nor ever so for the Church in the East during all the thousand years in union with the Roman Catholic Church. Their bishops, as a matter of fact, enjoyed a very wide autonomy and the Pope was simply the ultimate point of appeal for definitions of the faith and the protection of the basic Christian unity.

In the daily government of the Church, the Pope's areas of competence are vast and his influence over the entire Church is very strong. After the Second Vatican Council, however, the autonomy of the local church grew considerably and is, undoubtedly, destined for further development. History shows that the power of the Pope can be extended and restricted. On the one hand, it is balanced by the college of bishop and their responsibilities for the universal Church, and on the other, by the need of that same college of bishops always to be in union with the Pope.

The fact that the Holy See now enjoys an international juridical reality, that the Pope is Head of a State, however small and symbolic, and that he has diplomatic relations with governments – all this is the historical residue left over from a time when the Pope was a king. There are many useful aspects to this, for the Pope can carry out world wide initiatives in the cause of peace or in defence of weaker churches or those oppressed by authoritarian regimes. Many think, however, that the political position and the diplomatic aspect of the papacy detract from its freedom to preach the Gospel without compromise. One of the tasks of the Pope is to speak for the universal Church before the world and before history. What might be the best way of doing this, and what might be the most effective means of so doing, are obviously problems of considerable size and not easily resolved.

Chapter seven

Church and world: a difficult rapport

Christianity is an uprising of hope. We believe that God loves humanity and wants to save the world from pain and death. The Church is conscious of being both the bearer of this message to the world and also, in so far as the Church itself earnestly lives in fraternal union and is dedicated to the good of humanity and, above all, to the good of the poor, to some extent a realisation of this hope. But when will this saving plan of God truly come to pass? And how will it happen?

There are those among the faithful who live with a simple attitude of waiting: for them, the time of true salvation is yet to come. In this world, the Christian must just have faith, pray, frequent the sacraments and live honestly, and so he or she will earn Paradise and after his or her death they will experience the salvation of God. Others may have the presumption that the Church itself is the kingdom of God, that it is in this world with one task only: to convert people so that they join. People with this attitude observe the world cautiously, with a certain mistrust of all non-believers whom they see simply as lost to the Church.

There is, though, a third and different way of being in the world, in which the Church can find its place in society and in all that goes on there. This way springs from the conviction that salvation comes from God and that his designs are mysterious. We know the direction to move in only because it is revealed in the story of Jesus and made clear in his death and resurrection. In this sense, the Church (which knows Jesus) is conscious of having something to say to the world, but the world is not aware of this. It is not that the world's propositions have no value in the overarching plan of God; for Christ, risen and alive, has moved right into history. He has been sown once and for all, like an indestructible seed of the new creation. His presence is always at work among us, even in places where nobody knows about him and where his name is never heard. Through the power of this faith, the Church sees that the signs of the kingdom of God, revealed in Christ, are everywhere. It is necessary that the Church be immersed in the things of this world, that they live all mixed up together, that the Church interweave its own works with those of the world. But how is this to be done? How share where necessary and refute where necessary? How far can the Church go in identifying with the world, and at what point should it disengage itself from it?

In mission

God loved the world so much that he gave his Son, said Jesus and, speaking of the Holy Spirit, that we hear the Spirit like the wind which blows where it chooses, and we do not know where it comes from or where it is going (cf John 3). It is God who saves the world. The Spirit empowers people where and when he chooses, so the fate of people is not in the hands of us believers. Yet we do have something which the world does not, for we have the Good News of Jesus. We have heard about him. We know about his life, his deeds and his message and, above all, we believe that he is now all that he then was, we believe that he lives because he is risen.

For this reason, Christians are debtors to the world which they confront. Convinced that we do not save ourselves but that it is God who saves us, and open to discovering signs of the Holy Spirit who both goes before us and brings forth fruit at will, we can at least communicate to others what we ourselves have learned, namely, the Good News that Jesus is risen. In him we each find hope and salvation.

'Woe to me if I do not preach the gospel!' said St Paul in his first letter to the Christians at Corinth (1 Cor 9:16), and it is always like that for the Church everywhere in the world. The Christian community shares the earthly lot of the people among whom they live, they share in their joys and sufferings, their hopes and anguish. They give and they receive, but the fundamental debt they owe to everyone they meet is this, to share their faith in Jesus. There are a number of needs and problems resulting from this basic sharing which characterises the Church in this world, and these needs and problems give rise to some conflicts.

The risk of the absolute

The proclamation that Jesus, after he had lived among us and been brutally killed, is now risen is far from obvious. There is no way in which such a testimony can be given, heard or refuted, as if it were just an ordinary human communication. If everyone has some value in life which they consider a top priority – it might be their feelings, the family, professional success or simply money and enjoyment – the believer is one who has discovered a new value in among all these others. It is this: Jesus is risen and alive, he gave his life for our love. This is God's revelation: that he does not abandon us to ourselves but loves us. To have heard and believed this is like opening up the roof and seeing the stars.

This pure and simple affirmation of God, and this declaration that in Jesus, God has entered our history, put the Church in a different position from that of any other body of human endeavour. It inevitably means that the Church works from an inner intention, bearing something different, something which cannot be measured by the ordinary values by which we assess the facts of our existence. From this it follows that the Church looks at things with a certain diffidence, almost like a player who has an ace up his sleeve. So those who have no sense of a mysterious and divine 'something' coming to rest in our world consider it simply nonsense, an illusion people have set up but with little or no rational basis.

For many, it seems very strange to entrust our personal destiny and that of humanity to God. We have only to think of the impression that the Christian community will have on unbelieving pacifists when it organises a prayer vigil for peace. To pacifists, it seems absurd to seek peace from the Almighty, we must claim this from the mighty of the earth. The Church's life is sprinkled with such incommunicable aspects, and this brings its own burden of suffering. On the other hand, the world is being driven to open up its roof and discover the stars. In the very moment of observing that the Christian makes no sense, people can also ask whether the true meaning of life might, perhaps, be sought beyond the immediately significant, beyond the banal and everyday. So the absolute character of faith can provoke other dramas. In the eyes of the Church, Jesus, and only he, is Lord. The Christian community cannot avoid confrontation if it finds itself in a society which claims to impose absolute values of its own, values which are determined by custom or ideology, law or tradition. Sometimes this confrontation will be dramatic and violent.

The Church is prepared to share with the world in every service that people need. It is ready to go along with general policies from which the Church itself does not benefit. It is also ready to serve the world itself, to be at the disposal of scientific theory, of technology, ideology or politics when these are concerned with the future of humanity. The only qualification is that in the end, the Church must put all things under the ultimate judgement of the Lord Jesus. We recall what happened to the early Church in the Roman Empire. The Christians were no revolutionaries. In their letters, the apostles urged them to be exemplary citizens, obedient to authority. It is also true that the Roman Empire was extremely tolerant of the fact of religion. In that case, why was Christ not found in the Pantheon beside all the other gods? Why was Christianity alone, apart from Judaism, persecuted so bitterly and so tragically? Because although Christians were quite ready to obey the emperor and his laws, they were not ready to adore him as their god and saviour. This was not a ritual formality; fundamentally it was a political problem, because rejecting the divine nature of the emperor meant that Christians did not accept any absolute power over men and women, or their consciences, except that of the one Lord, the risen Jesus. The emperor saw, very perceptively, that at depth these meek and mild Christians were subversive, although they did not see themselves in that light. Every attempt to make humanity itself (or ideas, or systems, or things, or technical means, or political programmes) into an absolute value, inevitably runs up against the proclamation of the absolute character of God.

So the Church, from time to time, is called to the supreme test of martyrdom. At that moment, it lives out its most dramatic confrontation with the world and also renders the world its greatest service. It summons the world, in the name of God, to recognise the dignity and the freedom of humanity.

The risk of the relative

If God's part in the faith experience is an aspect quite beyond ordinary human evaluation, the other aspect, the human story of the believer struggling to leaven the bread of humanity with the power of faith, is easily assessed by the world, even if only critically. In fact, we must always remember that for the Church to proclaim Christ is to proclaim itself. There is no way the faith can be communicated without some sharing in the experience of it. What the risen Christ might be or might wish will be of no interest to those who have decided not to believe in him, but what the Church does in his name and how the Church lives among people is a matter of great interest to any who are in touch with a Christian community.

The historical experience of the Church is given life by its faith, but is not absolutely the same as that faith. Acts of faith are surrounded by the things people do in their ordinary lives. Faith is intertwined with all their actions, mingled in with them, so that sometimes it loses its particular identity altogether, and vanishes. Even though the Church bears within it the mystery of the Absolute, it still lives amid all the risks of human history. These include the possibility of being wrong, of being sinful or mistaken in specific ways. The divine presence in the Church says more about God than about the Church. This presence guarantees the endurance of faith in such a way that, right to the end of time, the Church will be able to bring people the news that Jesus has risen. It does not, however, give the Church a special, accident-free path on which to journey through history.

It follows from this that the Church must not only rely on the power of God's grace in order to fulfil its mission. It must also rely on ordinary criteria of human efficiency. Let us take the example of a Christian community which seeks to express its ideal of charity by founding a hospital. From the community's angle, we will be speaking about a valid faith experience if the sick are well cared for and often healed, but not if the community treat them by simply saying the rosary. In the same way, if Christians enter the political arena, they will not form good policies by favouring the interests of the Church. Their policies will be good only if they succeed in bringing about a just society where everyone's dignity and liberty are guaranteed. The Church would be falling into a kind of idolatry if, in its involvement with society, it put itself forward as the supreme standard of behaviour. This would bode as ill as when society is judged from any purely ideological standpoint, or when everything is subjected to a programme of economic, scientific or technological development. The criteria of historical efficiency, contingent and relative as they are, are asked of the Church when the community is called to the service of others or to the building of a better world. They are not asked of the Church when it is called to the absolute proclamation of the Lord, even though the Church is at the service of others, concerned in building a better world. So the Church finds itself living in the world, subject to historical tests of efficiency, but cannot claim acceptance by the world because of Jesus in whom the world does not believe. If the whole world believed, our problem would not exist. The Church must give its own evidence and then submit to the judgement of history. Does the Church serve human progress, or not? Do the Church's presence and activities serve the development of humanity, or not? Does the Church represent a force for progress or a hindrance in the construction of a better tomorrow for humanity?

The risk of the political

'The Church should not interfere with politics' is a statement as unfounded as it is frequent. How can a democratic society exclude some of its citizens from politics? It might be valid to do so with some aspects of the State, such as the army or the magistracy, but the Church is not an aspect of the State. On the other hand, the proclamation: Jesus is Lord, does imply a political principle. It amounts to saying that there is no other lordship and is therefore a proclamation of freedom. The main political clash between the Church and society arises from its criticisms of those who try to impose something as an absolute value. Middle-class ideology and mentality, for instance, make the laws of economics into absolute values. Market forces, the primacy of capital, the cult of money, the inviolability of private property – all these become idols. They affront the freedom offered us by the one Father, in whom everyone is an equal, everyone a brother or a sister. They affront the freedom offered by the one Lord, Jesus, who gave his life that all might live. Ideologies which make the nation the supreme value, which make the party the absolute guide in life or the radical freedom of the individual into the ultimate criterion of good, all these must not be surprised if they find the Church a constant conscientious objector.

The proclamation that Jesus is Lord means that ideological propositions are only acceptable as long as they are subject to the free judgement of conscience. It is a conviction of faith that Jesus is the God of creation, that he lives hidden in the hearts of us all and speaks through the voice of conscience, even through the consciences of those who do not believe in him. Where the party or the activities of the Stock Exchange, the results of the elections or a new work contract, class solidarity or the radical freedom of the individual, where these things try to take absolute command, then we are in the presence of a true and particular idolatry, setting itself up in competition with God.

The proclamation that Jesus is Lord is, as we have seen, a political reality, but it does not issue in some global organisation of social life nor in structures of State. However, the memory of Jesus and the way he thought about life, remains – the Christian inspiration. This is the ultimate appeal by which to judge any political project in which the Christian wants to engage. It means that the project must always take into account the human being, the one to whom God has given life. No matter what our political orientation, we must never make the person into an instrument. Politics must serve people, not make people servants.

So far we have considered the proclamation of certain relevant, fundamental political values. However, politics does not deal in grand principles so much as in concrete programmes, and the nature of these is to give society quick and precise ways of realising these programmes. All through history, the Church has given rise to a number of political ideologies. For instance, in the Middle Ages, the organisation of European society regulated its social life by Christian morality, trusting to the word and authority of the papacy, and to the temporal governance of the emperor. After the evangelisation of America, the Jesuits of Paraguay set up a Christian State which did away with private property and based itself on a sharing of goods inspired by the *Utopia* of St Thomas More and Campanella. These were the famous *Reductions* which, 150 years of life, were brutally wiped out by Portugal. Another Christian political ideology, admittedly only a partial one, was that which was set up in the year 800 in defence of the temporal power of the Church, that is, the Papal States. Another Christian political ideology is the principled rejection of the class war in the name of Christian solidarity: this seeks to construct a society in which the social classes temper their conflicting interests in pursuit of the common good, but without eroding their distinctive qualities.

No one should be surprised that Christianity and the Church give rise to projects and political movements. They are the natural consequence of the fact that, in addition to those aspects which come from the Lord, the mission of the Church is also lived out by serving humanity and within human history. These each impose different imperatives. The Church is called to proclaim Jesus as the only Lord. There is no political project, not even the most Christian and Catholic imaginable, which the Church could regard as an absolute value by which all the faithful could acceptably live; at least, not if they are to be considered faithful to the Gospel of Jesus. If the Church were to identify faith with an ideology or party, it would profoundly betray its awareness of its own mission, of the very meaning of the Church's political responsibility before the world.

Only Christians united in groups, associations, movements and parties can bring the mission of the Church to reality. This is effected when they share their faith with others, or put themselves at the service of others so as to bring about a more just and humane world. However, they must always remember that all these things are only part of the Church's faith experience; that is, their political work, belonging to a party, adopting different ways of resolving a particular social problem, setting up a political system, passing laws to safeguard human dignity. These things are relative, provisional, fallible and can be superseded. The Christian could never transform even one of them into an object of faith, or make it an indispensable condition for maintaining the communion of the Church.

The risk of inefficiency

Although the Church pursues something absolute and, in a certain sense, bears that absolute within itself, this does not free the Church from all the human risks of failure or of making mistakes.

When the Church embarks on serving humanity's earthly needs, it cannot rely on that absolute to guarantee earthly success. We all know that, at the level of history, the Church's success depends on its ability to be genuinely efficient.

There are, though, moments in which it must break with the criteria of efficiency. We have already seen this happen when assumptions are made on the world's side, of something absolute which is not Christ. In that case, the Church must choose martyrdom and death, the ultimate extreme of inefficiency. The Church's final destiny is salvation, it is the exaltation of the dignity and freedom of humanity, and these are bound up with the love of the one Lord, Jesus Christ. They may be surrendered to no other.

But apart from those moments when our affirmation of the absolute is at stake, there are other times when the imitation of Christ requires the Church to behave in a way that violates the canons of efficiency. Jesus is not the sort of exemplar who predetermines each and every specific action. His experience was human experience, and as such it was limited by the circumstances of time and place in which he lived. So he offers us some behavioural guidelines by which we break with the past and re-construct our lives on the original model. This enables us to express the novelty of his message and the change of focus he gives to human hope. At least two such examples emerge clearly from the Gospels: poverty and forgiveness of enemies.

The choice of poverty certainly does not mean a choice of efficiency, yet Christ requires it of his Church. The conflicts which are set up in the Christian community by this evangelical norm are well known, and in its dealings with the world, the Church often finds itself reproached for infidelity to Christ on just this point. Obviously, if we are to harmonise efficiency with evangelisation and the Church's activities in this world, then there will be problems. For instance, organising schools and hospitals or making use of postage stamps and radio, all require the Church to have and to use considerable wealth. Without large sums of money, missionaries cannot be sent all round the world. On a more modest scale, the administration of even a tiny parish and the organisation of even the smallest possible catechism class both require money. So how is the Church to love that poverty offered it by Christ, and demanded from it by Christ?

When Christians are involved in the struggle for justice, in trade unions and politics or, as sometimes happens, in the tragedy of revolution, how then are they to model their behaviour on Christ? In the end, it is probably not always possible to conduct efficient politics in a spirit of love for our enemies. Yet the difficulties do not cancel out those imperatives which we have received explicitly and directly from the Gospel.

In conclusion, it must be said that basically the Church's work in this world fully shares in the normal ebb and flow of all the other works of humanity. The Church is inextricably intertwined with these. From time to time, the Church will step out of line and will react unexpectedly. From time to time, it will shatter the criteria of efficiency and astonish all its travelling companions. This is the sign that the Church's hope still has dimensions which are new and different.

Chapter eight

Between the past and the future

The communion, which the believer longs to extend so that it is unbounded, is more than a geographic definition, more than a communion which includes different races and cultures.

It is also historical, stretching through the sequence of different times and epochs.

Apostolicity: a past

It is the custom of the Catholic Church to celebrate the memory of its saints, especially the apostles and martyrs of the first centuries and to give their names to babies. It is the custom to preserve ancient formulae with love and fidelity, even those which derive from the Old Testament and remotest times. In order to grasp the essential character of the Church, these phenomena can never be seen as simply casual or meaningless. In our culture and our civic life, we have very few expressions of historical memory to equal that of the Church. This is so much so that quite often young people rebel against it, either rejecting the Church as they throw would away a worn out overall, or else agitating from within for radical reform.

Yet historical memory is itself a form of communion, a communion between generations and epochs. It is a communion with those who have left the stage of this world and are now believers living in God. No Christian, no Church, would have the presumption to invent its own faith for itself, here and now to create its own Christ and to ignore the debt we owe to the generations who lived the faith before us. We have said, many times, that we must base our faith on the witness of the apostolic Church. This vital necessity is not peculiar to today's Church. Every generation of Christians has, in its time, been concerned to base its message faithfully on the message of the apostles. For this reason, the apostolicity of today's Church is not like a bridge leaping over the generations in between, so as to connect directly with the founding events. It is more like a thread running through the centre of all the various phases and experiences which make up history. The Church can ignore or skip nothing of its past.

This way of thinking about the apostolicity of the Church could seem conservative and reactionary, neither can we forget that the Church's history contains moments, episodes and aspects of which the serious Christian can only be ashamed. There are a number of pages in the Church's annals which one would dearly love to tear out. Anticlericals or polemicists against the Church will throw in our faces such episodes as the condemnation of Galileo, the crusades, Alexander VI, the burnings at the stake, the Inquisition. It is important to realise that communion with the Church of the past does not mean a blanket approval of all that happened.

The principle of discernment lies in looking back to the apostolic witness. If it is true that where the faith is, there the Holy Spirit is creating the Church, then we must acknowledge that if faith survives among us, then it must mean that the Holy Spirit has not abandoned the Church. If the Spirit had gone, then no one today would believe in Jesus. No reform can be based on a dead and empty past. Instead, the Church has this history always in mind, to refer to and to learn from, in order to find a way forward. This is an important problem and we should attend to it. If, in the name of the apostles, we had the right to step out of the history of the Church and ignore all that has happened since their time, then the next generations could also abstract themselves from the Christian experience that we are living and developing today. Then there would be neither a Church of the past nor a Church of the future. We would have nothing to say or contribute to the Church's tomorrow. Neither would we have anything to offer the future of the world. Christianity tomorrow, on such an hypothesis, would only have its remotest origins to refer back to and there would be nothing of the generations between – just the destruction of all communion between the Church and times and ages past.

Apostolicity: a future

The apostolic tradition creates a critical continuity between successive generations of Christians. It is an austere communion, neither rhetorical nor triumphalist. In chapter 19 of his Gospel, St Matthew relates a curious dialogue between Jesus and his apostles. They are reminding him that they have left everything in order to follow him, and are demanding to know what their reward will be. Jesus says that when the world is renewed and Christ has become its ultimate Judge and Lord, they will sit on 12 thrones and judge the 12 tribes of Israel. In other words, by their witness to faith, they will have become a permanent tribunal at whose bar the Church, the new Israel, must submit its history. For Jesus, the apostolic tradition is far from being a way of enclosing the Church in its past, or of turning it into a kind of archive keeping documents about its own origin. Quite the contrary, it is precisely through a return to its beginnings that the Church begins to be renewed. The apostolic Church, where our roots are, judges us, and measures the distance between us and the ideal. It is this that urges us to keep journeying forward in search of new, purer and richer patterns to live by, patterns through which we can proclaim our faith to the world.

To say that our Church is apostolic is a way of naming the dynamic which has moved it throughout history. It is neither a Church without a past nor a Church without a future. It is its apostolic origin that makes the Church unique in time. It is a most ancient organism, so complete that even at in its moments of greatest decadence it is being reborn, it is rediscovering itself and is able, yet again, to reconstruct its authentic face.

Conservative and progressive

The Church always has a problem siting itself accurately within history. Apostolicity is its guiding thread, but it is not an automatic solution. There is a tension between the perspectives of the past and those of the future and this generates tension between those who wave the flag of the past and those who agitate for ceaseless renewal.

The conservative tendency of the Church begins with unexceptionable data. The absolute norm for the Church is found in the faith of the past, in the event of Jesus to which the apostles bore witness and which they set down definitively in Sacred Scripture. These basic facts, which are beyond argument, become immeasurably amplified when subsequent events are seen as an infallible extension of the original event, and therefore as something no longer subject to discernment or renewal. Minor traditions, which are often simply from 'the good old days' of the recent past, are aligned on the apostolic succession no less. The old becomes the ancient; tradition becomes The Tradition. Our childhood memories replace the memory of the Church, and all the little things to which Christians or communities are sentimentally attached become raised up to the status of the normative events which began the Church. Quite logically, the conservative tendency is authoritarian. It aspires to incarnate tradition with such massive continuity that it need no longer submit itself to the authority of Christ or the apostolic Church. What is more, the conservative has a dream even about civil society, the dream of a State in which the Church makes all the laws, exactly as if it had become a true incarnation of God. The government, then, would simply apply Christian principles to specific cases and all the citizens would faithfully obey.

The progressive tendency, on the other hand, sees history as continuous movement. In order to build a better future for humanity, the Church must be inserted into this movement. Everything the progressives say and do tries to serve a more just and beautiful

100

tomorrow. With this line of thought, it is difficult to maintain any sense of faith as obedience to a Word from above – from God – that is, brought to us who were far off by Jesus and his apostles. This word imposes itself beyond any values I, we, this whole generation, might have about a historical efficiency in which we have done well. On the other hand, it is interesting to notice that, generally speaking, traditionalists do not much care for the Bible, while progressives love it. The traditionalists seem to perceive the Word of God in the established structures, almost to the extent of eliminating ancient history and making the Church begin in the recent past or the present. The progressives seem to leap over the past and the present, looking to the earliest beginnings for their inspiration for the future.

These tensions, which the Church has to carry and live with, are an accurate expression of that disquiet which is, in the end, the Church's wealth. The Church does have a future, it exists for the future of the world, but the Church is not the finishing post. It is a sign, an indication, a trace of the world's path towards the kingdom of God. To try and block this movement by embalming the Church, making it the measure of all things and tying down others' evolution to its own paralysed condition, is an act of idolatry. This is what happens when the Church usurps the place of its Lord. But, again, to immerse the Church in the world's movement towards its future does not mean consigning it into the hands of the first wizard who comes along pretending to hold the secret of the future in his own ideology. The risen Lord is the future of the world, and he is inscrutable in his mystery. This is why the Church feels, and must feel, free from involvement in programmes of history. It must retain the courage to be useless while its own hope moves it beyond all those schemes in which others try to involve it.

I do not believe that the resolution of the conservative-progressive tension will come through compromise – a little movement forward but not too much, preserving the past but with certain cards kept up the sleeve. It is more important to know when the Church is compromising itself, to know when it can fearlessly surrender to the tides of history and when such a surrender would compromise the absolute priority of the Lord. Quite simply, the Church does not exist apart from the Word of God, and the Church knows this. It is the Word of God which keeps the Church far more than the Church which keeps the Word of God. There are matters which and moments when everyone can and must change constantly. There are matters on which and moments when we need to dig in our heels, regardless of how hard we may be pushed from above. There are matters which and moments when, in our obedience, we submit only to God, not to people. To know how to recognise and distinguish these matters and moments from each other is a gift to beseech the Spirit to bestow on us.

Infallible

The Church, then, bears within itself the absolute word of God. So can the Church never be wrong? Only God is never wrong. The Church makes mistakes, but it is impossible for the Church to be always mistaken. The First Vatican Council, which closed in 1870, by declaring that the Pope is infallible, lit a match and set it to a problem far wider than the person of the Pope. This is something which concerns the entire Church in its possibility of truly being the *locus* of faith in the world.

We can speak of Christ in many different ways, and everyone wants to say authentic things in his or her own way. In the end, one person says that Christ is God, another that he is not, one that Christ is truly human and another that he is an apparition of God in human form, one that we must forgive our enemies and another that we must hate them – not at all the same thing.

It is true that faith and the imperative of conscience are interior realities and not just words. So it can happen that someone may express the faith perfectly but have no interior belief at all. Contrariwise, another may express the faith clumsily but be living by something very authentic in his or her heart. It can also happen that someone observes the Gospel precepts outwardly while his or her heart is far from God; while another can, in good faith, give himself or herself to an ideal which is not truly evangelical. The impossibility of establishing an exact nexus between the inner reality and the exterior expression does not, alas, eliminate the problem. Faith is not simply an interior matter. If it comes through communication from another, then it is also an external fact. True faith can hide under a false expression of faith, and an act hostile to the Gospel can be done in good conscience. But could the profession of a false creed and the preaching of a non-Christian morality ever bring the apostolic Church to birth? Let us imagine that at some point, all the words the Church has used to express the faith became false, and all the norms by which we evaluated a programme of life were somehow no longer evangelical. At this point we would have to say that there is no longer a Church. Would we then have to face the fact that the

Church had died before the world had fulfilled its destiny, contrary though this is to the promises of Christ? If this is unthinkable, then we must believe that the Holy Spirit will sustain the truth of the Church, and not permit mistakes, at least in the essential articulation of the Church's message. The Church absolutely could not live and bear witness to the world if it were always apprehensive, fearing that the proclamation of the risen Jesus, its one Lord, would one day be shown up as untrue.

The ways of expressing the faith and interpreting Gospel life are many and various and may even be contradictory – as long as they rest on the essential basis of the message and as long as they do not compromise this message. The ways the essential substance of the message is formulated will vary from one generation to another; they are constantly being refined, enriched and made a better fit for an evolving culture and changing human situations. But at the moment when the Church denies them as mistaken, then we will have to admit that the Church is no more. Such a time would be in need of a new creation of God; for the Church would be without a history, without the apostles, without past and without future.

So the Church preserves a Creed, handed down to it through the spontaneous developments of the Church's expression of faith, as well as through the debates of the first councils. Through 2,000 years' experience of faith, the Church knows what it needs if it is to exist as the authentic apostolic Church. In this process lies the gift of infallibility. This gift is lived spontaneously by the people of God, and is present explicitly in the councils and the Popes. Until the road of faith arrives at its goal, the pastors of the Church will guide it and allow its daily expressions of belief to move through spontaneous changes. When the diversity becomes so great that it no longer expresses the same Christ but instead begins to split open the essential witness of faith, then the bishops will urge the Pope to speak the authoritative word of the one faith. Given life by the Spirit, the Church believes that the Lord, who has called it to be a sign of the kingdom of God throughout history, will give it this true and infallible word. It is a necessary word if its mission is not to dissolve into nothing.

The normal life of the Church flows, obviously, without constant appeal to this exceptional moment of grace. The normal riches of the Church lie in pluralism and the evolution of its word. Sin and error put it on guard against presumption, working on it and making it share fully in the normal journey of human history. When the heart of the Church feels separated from the witness of faith by which it lives, then it returns to the rock on the which Christ wanted it to be solidly based, namely the infallible word of faith spoken in the ecumenical councils and by the Pope. These are, obviously, exceptional moments. As a fact of history, such infallible pronouncements have seldom been made. In the councils of the first centuries we have the credal formulations about the Trinity of God and the person of Christ. In the Council of Trent there were the definition of the seven sacraments, and the definition about the biblical canon and tradition. The most recent exercise of the Papal magisterium has been that of the dogmas about Mary. In the last Council, Vatican II, there was so much material put forward about the doctrine and practice of ecclesial life that they said explicitly that the bishops did not want to make any infallible definitions.

Infallibility is a gift of the Spirit to the Church, not

given to free it from the risks of life but to preserve the Gospel for the world. The Church can certainly make mistakes. Mistakes can even be maintained for quite some time, but they cannot last, they cannot deform the message of salvation which has been delivered to the Church by Jesus for the men and women of all the generations of history.

Chapter nine

An everyday road

And in the Spirit he carried me away to a great, high mountain, and showed me the holy city Jerusalem coming down out of heaven from God, having the glory of God, its radiance like a most rare jewel, like a jasper, clear as crystal. It had a great, high wall, with twelve gates... and on the gates the names of the twelve tribes of the sons of Israel were inscribed... and the wall of the city had twelve foundations, and on them the twelve names of the twelve apostles of the Lamb. ... And the twelve gates were twelve pearls, each of the gates made of a single pearl, and the street of the city was pure gold, transparent as glass. And I saw no temple in the city, for its temple is the Lord God the Almighty and the Lamb... And its lamp is the Lamb (Rev 21:10-14.21-23).

In the vision of the apostle John, recounted in the last book of the New Testament, the Apocalypse, there is this dream of a Church of perfect splendour, a Church as it will be when the new heaven and the new earth have come. Here and now, on this earth and under these skies, the piazzas of the Church do not shine as splendidly as crystal, because they are trodden by people with muddy shoes. We need a sanctuary in which to discover the presence of God, because our eyes are dim and we do not notice God there where he is, which is everywhere. We still need the light of the sun by day and that of the moon by night because that light which comes from within our hearts has to penetrate through our all too opaque bodies.

Because it is founded on the apostles, of whom some were fishermen, the Church loves the image of itself as a ship. There is an episode recounted in the Gospel, in which there was a tempest on the lake but Jesus went on sleeping peacefully in the boat. The agitated apostles woke him up and he calmed the storm, but then he reproached: "where is your faith?" This is a temptation the faithful know all too well: for it does sometimes seems as if this story prefigured the Church's situation, we too have a sense that Jesus is asleep while the boat is going down.

To live in the Church is to experience those moments of great joy and fresh enthusiasm which come when we are sharing our hope with this world which so thirsts for such a hope, or when we build signs of community in the name of Jesus, or rejoice in sharing the communion of brothers and sisters. We also know moments of loss and great uncertainty. Jesus gave us no promises that he would never sleep in the boat again while the tempest raged. There are also moments in which it seems that he is again being crucified and that, this time, the tomb is finally closed.

Yet in truth, he is not asleep or dead in the tomb. When fear takes hold of us or we are sinful, it seems that he cannot still be alive and near us. However, the

Church with gates of pearl and strong, high walls is already here, even though it be hidden in a community which believes but has no splendour at all.

Graham Greene, in a famous novel called *The Power and the Glory*, tells the story of a priest who was being hunted by the police during the Thirty Years' Mexican persecution. He was an alcoholic, he had lived with a woman, but he was the only priest left in the area. One of his sermons, heavy with the sense of his misery and his fidelity, can worthily close these reflections of ours on the Church:

> It was dark: no sign as yet of the dawn. Perhaps two dozen people sat on the earth floor of the largest hut while he preached to them. He said, 'One of the Fathers has told us that joy always depends on pain. Pain is part of joy. We are hungry and then think how we enjoy our food at last. We are thirsty ...' He stopped suddenly, with his eyes glancing away into the shadows, expecting the cruel laugh that did not come. He felt his own unworthiness like a weight at the back of the tongue. 'That is why I tell you that heaven is here: this is a part of heaven just as pain is a part of pleasure.' Literary phrases from what seemed now to be another life altogether – the strict quiet life of the seminary – became confused on his tongue: the names of precious stones: Jerusalem the Golden. But these people had never seen gold.
>
> He went rather stumbling on, 'Heaven is where there is no *jefe*, no unjust laws, no taxes, no soldiers and no hunger. Your children do not die in heaven... Oh, it is easy to say all the things that there will *not* be in heaven: what is there is God. That is more difficult. Our words are made to describe what we know with our senses. We say 'light', but we are

thinking only of the sun, 'love'... It was not easy to concentrate: the police were not far away. This is what he was used to: the words not striking home, the hurried close, the expectation of pain coming between him and his faith. He said stubbornly, "Above all remember this – heaven is here." Were they on horseback or on foot? If they were on foot, he had twenty minutes left to finish Mass and hide. 'Here now, at this minute, your fear and my fear are part of heaven, where there will be no fear any more for ever.'